Rekindling *the* Fire

A Devotional on
Returning to The Father's Refining Fire
and Who He Created You To Be

John W. Nichols

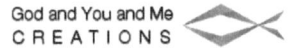

Rekindling the Fire: A Devotional on Returning to
The Father's Refining Fire and Who He Created You To Be
Copyright © 2025 by John W. Nichols.

All rights reserved. Printed in the United States of America. No part of this book may be used or reproduced in any manner whatsoever without written permission except in the case of brief quotations embodied in critical articles or reviews.

Published in Shenandoah, Texas, by God and You and Me CREATIONS.
For information contact : John@GodAndYouAndMe.com

Edited by Joanne Hillman, www.JoanneHillman.com
and Victoria Quigley

Cover design and Book Formatting by John Nichols
www.GodAndYouAndMe.com/BookHelp

Cover art by Cooper, George. [Illustration of a lamp]. (1806). The Miriam and Ira D. Wallach Division of Art, Prints and Photographs: Art & Architecture Collection, The New York Public Library. "A Design for a branch light, proposed to be executed in silver." The New York Public Library Digital Collections. 1806.

Special thanks to Pure Fire Ministries for providing the use of their flame logo for the cover of the book.
www.PureFireMinistries.org.

Scripture quotations marked AMP are taken from the Amplified® Bible, Copyright © 2015 by The Lockman Foundation. Used by permission. www.Lockman.org

Scripture quotations marked AMPC are taken from the Amplified® Bible, Copyright © 1954, 1958, 1962, 1964, 1965, 1987 by The Lockman Foundation. Used by permission. www.Lockman.org

Scripture quotations marked NASB are taken from the New American Standard Bible®, Copyright © 1960, 1962, 1963, 1968, 1971, 1972, 1973, 1975, 1977, 1995 by The Lockman Foundation. Used by permission. www.Lockman.org

Scripture quotations marked NKJV are taken from the New King James Version®. Copyright © 1982 by Thomas Nelson. Used by permission. All rights reserved.

Scripture quotations marked NLT are taken from the Holy Bible, New Living Translation, copyright © 1996, 2004, 2015 by Tyndale House Foundation. Used by permission of Tyndale House Publishers, Inc., Carol Stream, Illinois 60188. All rights reserved.

Scripture quotations marked TPT are from The Passion Translation®. Copyright © 2017, 2018 by Passion & Fire Ministries, Inc. Used by permission. All rights reserved. ThePassionTranslation.com.

Translations of Hebrew and Greek words taken from Strong's Exhaustive Concordance, Copyright © 1890 by James Strong, S.T.D., LL.D. Public Domain.

Dictionary quotations marked Webster's 1828 Dictionary are from Noah Webster, American Dictionary of the English Language, 1828. Public Domain.

Print Edition March 2025 ISBN: 978-1-7328093-5-2
Kindle Edition March 2025 ASIN: Coming Soon
10 9 8 7 6 5 4 3 2 1

A Devotional on
Returning to the Father's Refining Fire
and Who He Created You To Be

REKINDLING the FIRE

JOHN W. NICHOLS

*For every burning heart that has gone dim,
who yearns for the fire to start again.*

Contents

Introduction 1

Day 1: Returning to the Father 9

Day 2: Repentance, Renunciation, & Laying Down Your Life . 19

Day 3: Willing to be a Slave, but with a Son's Mindset 27

Day 4: Removing Previous Identities and Cleansing with Water 35

Day 5: Only One Master 43

Day 6: The Warfare of Capturing Thoughts and Tearing Down Strongholds 53

Day 7: Preparing the Soul to Receive 61

Day 8: Meeting with the King in the Secret Place 71

Day 9: Anointed for Consecration 79

Day 10: Infilling of His Presence 89

Day 11: Rekindling the Fire 99

Day 12: Clothed for Celebration 109

Day 13: Worshiping in Spirit and Truth 117

Day 14: Restored as a Beloved Child 125

Day 15: Living as the Son 135

Day 16: Joyful Satisfaction in Him 143

Day 17: Manifesting the Holy Spirit 155

Day 18: Burning Bright 167

Day 19: Becoming Sensitive to the Spirit 177

Day 20: Changing the World 189

Day 21: Looking Forward 201

Additional Notes 213

Free Stuff! 217

About the Author 219

Introduction

"I advise you to buy from Me gold refined by fire so that you may become rich, and white garments so that you may clothe yourself, and that the shame of your nakedness will not be revealed; and eye salve to anoint your eyes so that you may see. Those whom I love, I reprove and discipline; therefore be zealous and repent."

REVELATION 3:18-19 NASB

"For the Lord corrects those He loves, just as a father corrects a child in whom he delights."

PROVERBS 3:12 NLT

CAN YOU BE a prodigal child and not realize it? Can you be a prodigal attending church? Can you serve God while being a prodigal son? Can you be a teacher, evangelist, pastor, prophet, or apostle and also be a prodigal? When I was a missionary overseas, and one of a group of pastors in an international church, serving and giving with all that I had, authoring books about Christian faith, praying and preaching regularly, seeing the Holy Spirit move through me, Jesus called me a prodigal. In the secret place, as I was waiting on Him, I heard His familiar voice, and was shocked.

You probably picked up this book, not because you have run away from God, but because you want to rekindle that first love that initially turned around your whole life. Bear with me and try not to be offended. Jesus showed me that it's possible to be a prodigal son even while doing all the "right" things. As we see in Revelation 3:18-19 above, Fatherly discipline is a part of the refining fire promised by the title of this book. And by the way, I am not only speaking to men when I mention prodigal sons and sonship. Whoever places their faith in Christ becomes a son of God.

> *There is neither Jew nor Greek, there is neither slave nor free, there is neither male nor female; for you are all one in Christ Jesus.*
> GALATIANS 3:28 NKJV
> (SEE ALSO ROMANS 8:14-17)

Both men and women can become prodigal sons, and both need their heavenly Father's pruning. As I learned over a year and a half ago, it's quite shocking to be called a prodigal when you think you're close to the Father. But Jesus knows what we need to really come to terms with what has made us dull, cooled our passions, and stolen our hearts from Him.

We think of the expression, "prodigal son," as being someone who has left the faith, or who was raised up attending a Christian church but is now separated from the Church-body. This makes sense as we read the parable Jesus preaches in Luke 15:11-32. But without disregarding that conclusion, let's look at it from another angle and see if there is more for us to glean. I believe we can use this parable to help us fan again into flames the holy fire of God in our hearts.

We'll jump into scripture and some of my own commentary below, but first let's look at the definition according to Webster's 1828 Dictionary:

> *"PROD'IGAL, noun. One that expends money extravagantly or without necessity; one that is profuse or lavish; a waster; a spendthrift."*

Now we'll read what Jesus says in Luke 15:11-24 (NKJV), and I'll break it down:

> *[11] Then He said: "A certain man had two sons. [12] And the younger of them said to his father, 'Father, give me the portion of goods that falls to me.' So he divided to them his livelihood.*

We see here the setup for the prodigal son to receive the wealth which he ends up lavishly spending in a manner consistent with Webster's definition. This is also normally looked at as an allegory for people who grew up receiving the things of the faith. Now I'm going to take it further and include people who have gained the kingdom, the anointing, the spiritual gifts, the position, the fulfillment of God's call on their life.

> *[13] And not many days after, the younger son gathered all together, journeyed to a far country, and there wasted his possessions with prodigal*

living.

It makes sense to use this passage to apply to people who have grown out of church, or even their Christian faith. But I believe that Jesus showed me we can apply this also to people who wholeheartedly followed God and were entrusted with much, but somewhere along the way stopped relying on Him. They have taken the inheritance, but for some reason lost connection with the Father. Now the gifts are being expressed and the office operated in wastefully because God is no longer the source or the head. Though they may be "close" to Him, a part of them has fallen away, been deceived, grown cold, and lost zeal. After receiving so much from the Father, they got comfortable and broke away from a true dependence on Him.

[14] But when he had spent all, there arose a severe famine in that land, and he began to be in want.

We hope and pray that the ones who have left the church will come to see their lack and need. I'm also praying for the ones who remain in the church to examine their lives and discover they're operating on fumes, running out of oil, eating yesterday's daily bread, and continuing to store rotten manna. They can only last so long without digging deep again. I hate to admit this, but I have been here many times, and I think there are many other Christian leaders in this position too.

[15] Then he went and joined himself to a citizen of that country, and he sent him into his fields to feed swine. [16] And he would gladly have filled his

> *stomach with the pods that the swine ate, and no one gave him anything.*

The traditional back-slidden Christian/prodigal son needs to know that anything they can get for themselves apart from God will never satisfy. And the apostle, pastor, prophet, teacher, or evangelist needs to know that his own ability, understanding, and strength is a poor substitute for drawing from the vine of Christ. Where theology, preparation, perceived order, and "excellence" is controlling the environment in which the Holy Spirit wants to move freely, we have to recognize we are in a severe lack of the manifest presence of God.

> [17] *"But when he came to himself, he said, 'How many of my father's hired servants have bread enough and to spare, and I perish with hunger!"* [18] *"I will arise and go to my father, and will say to him, "Father, I have sinned against heaven and before you,"* [19] *"and I am no longer worthy to be called your son. Make me like one of your hired servants."*

Those mothers and fathers of lost sheep long for the day that their child will come to their senses and humbly return to the Shepherd. But how many of the parents have also lost the fire in the chapel where they pray and wait? Do they need to humble themselves and join again as bond-servants to Christ? I pray too that the shepherds in the church will fall on their faces, and cry out to return to their first love.

> [20] *"And he arose and came to his father. But when he was still a great way off, his father saw him and had compassion, and ran and fell on his neck and kissed him. [21] And the son said to him, 'Father, I have sinned against heaven and in your sight, and am no longer worthy to be called your son.'"*

When we turn to the right direction, whether we are in the midst of serving in church or the depths of worldly depravity, the Father's mercies are new every morning. As we take action steps back to the Father, He will surprise us with His love. In the first week of this devotional, we will be going over topics which fit into verses 17-21 of the parable.

> [22] *"But the father said to his servants, 'Bring out the best robe and put it on him, and put a ring on his hand and sandals on his feet. [23] And bring the fatted calf here and kill it, and let us eat and be merry; [24] for this my son was dead and is alive again; he was lost and is found.' And they began to be merry."*

Coming again under the Father's loving discipline and correction makes way for the refining fire in our lives. Then He is able to restore our identity, placing white raiment of righteousness on us, the signet ring of joint-heirship with the Son, and the shoes of the gospel of peace. Even as all the angels in heaven rejoice when a sinner repents, God also celebrates the coming back to life of the dead in the church with blessings of provision, favor, and destiny.

Whatever your story is, I am sure you can stand to grow closer to the Father, to remove more of what's holding you back, to zealously live out your identity in greater measure, and experience more of God's blessing in your life. That's ultimately what this book is about. And both the one who has deliberately turned away from the Father, as well as the one who has remained but grown cold, can receive.

Get These Free Resources

Free Stuff!

| Simple Steps to Hearing God | Walk with God, Change the World | Revolutionize Your Quiet Time |

Subscribe at: GodAndYouAndMe.com/rekindling-fire-free-stuff

- *God is Trying to Tell You Something.* An audio teaching in MP3 format, focused on the key to hearing God, common ways God speaks, and practical steps to hear Him today.
- *7 Keys to a Successful Time of Devotion to God.* A PDF with steps to include in your quiet time.
- *Navigating the Maze of Life with God.* A 60 page PDF about giving your life to God, being filled with the Holy Spirit, and walking in the power of

the Holy Spirit to live the life God intended you to live.
- Additional content only available to subscribers on GodAndYouAndMe.com. You can unsubscribe at any time and I promise not to spam you.

Get these free resources here. Most phones are capable of using the camera app to follow this link. Simply open the camera on your phone and point it at the page:

GodAndYouAndMe.com/Rekindling-Fire-Free-Stuff

Day 1:

RETURNING TO THE FATHER

For you have not received a spirit of slavery leading again to fear [of God's judgment], but you have received the Spirit of adoption as sons [the Spirit producing sonship] by which we [joyfully] cry, "Abba! Father!"

ROMANS 8:15 AMP

THIS MORNING I slowly read all of Romans 8. No matter how many times I've read it, I continue to drink from this deep well. I encourage you also to take in each verse afresh.

I have never stopped praying but there have been periods when I haven't felt connected to God. Times like these require a standing on the firm foundation of the Bible. Our feelings and even the "truth" of our circumstances must ultimately bow down to the Word of God.

When the prodigal son hit rock bottom, he thought it would be better to humble himself, return, and be a slave in his father's house (Luke 15:11-32—read the Introduction to understand why this will be referenced often). I must admit that my quiet internal prayers have probably sounded more like an abused slave than a son lately, but according to Romans 8:15 that's not the spirit God intended us to have. So I recognize something inside needs to be flipped on its head.

In many Middle Eastern cultures, "abba" is a word children use to call their dad. And in the Gospels, we read of Jesus addressing His Heavenly Father in this familiar way. Because of His sacrifice, we are also children of God and fellow heirs with Christ (verse 17). So when we find our hearts distant from the Lover of our souls, He's not looking for a groveling servant, but a son with a change of heart.

Coming to God without Guilt or Shame (and Our Part)

> *There is therefore now no condemnation to those who are in Christ Jesus, who do not walk according to the flesh, but according to the Spirit.*
> ROMANS 8:1 NKJV

The first four verses of Romans 8 contain the promise that, because of Christ, we do not have to be perfect and fulfill God's commands in our own strength and righteousness. We can come to Him absolutely free of shame and guilt. This is great news, and we need to really receive it. His abundant grace allows us to come to Him despite our failures, and it also empowers us to change.

We see a glimpse of that empowerment in the 2nd half of Romans 8:1. Many people pass over this condition. The promise of Jesus's fulfillment of the law is working in us who live not in the ways of this world, but the ways of the Holy Spirit (verses 3-4). The ability to live this way only comes by grace through faith.

As you read the chapter, look for both God's promises and your own responsibility. Without any religious pressure, I hope to encourage you to consider and obey what the Holy Spirit is prompting you to do as you read these. Be fully confident that you are able to accomplish every task that is your responsibility. You will know what these are as you read them. And again, be assured that everything He asks you to do is possible (with His help).

But if you fail, remind yourself these words:

> *Who will bring charges against God's elect? God is the one who justifies; who is the one who condemns? Christ Jesus is He who died, but rather, was raised, who is at the right hand of God, who also intercedes for us. Who will separate us from the love of Christ? Will tribulation, or trouble, or persecution, or famine, or nakedness, or danger, or sword?*
>
> *... For I am convinced that neither death, nor life, nor angels, nor principalities, nor things present, nor things to come, nor powers, nor height, nor depth, nor any other created thing will be able to separate us from the love of God that is in Christ Jesus our Lord.*
>
> ROMANS 8:33-35, 38-39 NASB
> (36-37 SKIPPED FOR BREVITY)

Even in the midst of our weakness, and the many arrows from our enemy, we can be confident in our Heavenly Father's justification and enduring love. When the prodigal son again approached the kingdom he had rejected, his Father ran to meet him, celebrated his return, and restored him completely. We must have revelation from this parable that our Abba loves us incomprehensibly more than we can understand.

His Good Plan

> *And we know that God causes everything to work together for the good of those who love God and are called according to His purpose for them. For God knew His people in advance, and He chose them to become like His Son, so that His Son would be the firstborn among many brothers and sisters. And having chosen them, He called them to come to Him. And having called them, He gave them right standing with himself. And having given them right standing, He gave them His glory.*
> ROMANS 8:28-30 NLT

You may have heard these verses or paraphrases of them quoted a million times, but do your best to wipe the slate clean and internalize them anew. Imagine what your life would look like if you really believed with all your heart these God-breathed words. Start to treat your Heavenly Father as your Abba, and walk in your identity as His child again.

Pray today:

> *Abba, I humbly return to You. I separate myself from the worldly things that have drawn me away, and thanks to*

the blood of Your precious Son, I come out of all condemnation. I am making a declaration that I am turning away from the world, and coming into the tangible presence of my Father. Thank You that Your mercies are new daily, Your love never fails, and You restore me to sonship. Thank You for the wonderful promises in Your Word. Please help me apprehend them by grace through faith. I have found my knowledge and even my beliefs to not be enough. Awaken my heart to be able to receive these truths in a new way. I don't want to just know about Your good plans for me and my inheritance in Christ. I want to live it out. I seek to tap into the deepest fountain of living water, that Your Spirit would gush out and overflow, empowering this life to look like Jesus. So be it, according to Your Word!

Journaling prompt:

I have summarized key promises and responsibilities from Romans 8 below. As you read them, notice the ones the Holy Spirit highlights for you. Address your journal to God, asking Him to help you again receive each promise and act on the responsibilities in faith.

Responsibilities (paraphrased from Romans 8 NKJV):

- Being in Christ
- Do not walk/live according to the flesh
- Walk/live according to the Spirit
- Do not set your mind on the things of the flesh, but on the things of the Spirit

- Do not be carnally minded, but be spiritually minded
- Do not be in the flesh but in the Spirit
- If by the Spirit you put to death the deeds of the body, you will live
- We are children of God, heirs of God, and joint heirs with Christ, if indeed we suffer with Him, that we may also be glorified together
- If we hope for what we do not see, we eagerly wait for it with perseverance
- We are to love God and follow His calling

Promises (paraphrased from Romans 8 NKJV):

- No condemnation
- Being in Christ
- Free from the law of sin and death
- The righteous requirement of the law might be fulfilled in us
- Being spiritually minded is life and peace
- The Spirit of God dwells in you
- The body is dead because of sin, but the Spirit is life because of righteousness, and if the Spirit of Him who raised Jesus from the dead dwells in you, He also gives life to your mortal bodies through His Spirit
- If by the Spirit you put to death the deeds of the body, you will live
- For as many as are led by the Spirit of God, these are sons of God

- You did not receive the spirit of bondage again to fear, but you received the Spirit of adoption by whom we cry out, "Abba, Father."
- The Spirit Himself bears witness with our spirit that we are children of God, and if children, then heirs of God and joint heirs with Christ
- We may also be glorified together with Christ
- The sufferings of this present time are not worthy to be compared with the glory which shall be revealed in us, which creation eagerly waits for
- The creation will be delivered from the bondage of corruption into the glorious liberty of the children of God
- We have the fruit of the Spirit, and eagerly wait for the adoption, the redemption of our body
- The Spirit helps in our weaknesses
- The Spirit Himself makes intercession for us, according to the will of God
- All things work together for good to those who love God, called according to His purpose
- He foreknows us, and predestines us to be conformed to the image of His Son
- He also calls, justifies, and glorifies us
- God is for us; therefore who can be against us
- He gave His own Son for us all, and He will also freely give us all things
- Christ, at the right hand of God, makes intercession for us
- Neither tribulation, distress, persecution, famine,

nakedness, peril, or sword; neither death nor life, angels, principalities, powers, things present nor things to come, height nor depth, nor any other created thing, shall be able to separate us from the love of God which is in Christ Jesus our Lord
- In all these things we are more than conquerors through Him who loved us

_____
_____
_____
_____
_____
_____
_____
_____
_____
_____
_____
_____
_____
_____
_____
_____
_____
_____
_____
_____
_____
_____

John W. Nichols

Day 2:

Repentance, Renunciation, & Laying Down Your Life

> *"If you want to be my disciple, you must, by comparison, hate everyone else—your father and mother, wife and children, brothers and sisters— yes, even your own life. Otherwise, you cannot be my disciple. And if you do not carry your own cross and follow me, you cannot be my disciple... you cannot become my disciple without giving up everything you own."*
>
> Luke 14:26-27, 30 NLT

THE ABOVE QUOTE can be found within quite a large section of "red letters," where Jesus says and teaches many things including the parable of the Prodigal Son in the next chapter. As a large crowd began to follow Him, He turned to them and made it clear that He is to be absolutely first in His followers' lives. Everything else, even good things, must be secondary.

This means whatever is coming between you and Him has to go.

Turning Away from All that is Holding You Back

You have probably heard Romans 6:23, "For the wages of sin is death, but the gracious gift of God is eternal life in Christ Jesus our Lord (NASB)." We primarily think of this verse in the evangelistic context, which is good. But even after you have been born again, and you are destined for heaven, the wages of sin continue to be death.

We should not tread on God's grace, neither by continuing in obvious sins of commission or omission, or by allowing anything to become an idol. If your heart has placed something above Jesus, it has become a little god in your life. One that brings a little death. And although eternal life is a gift, truly allowing Jesus to be Lord in your life requires all those household gods to fall on their faces and be destroyed.

> *Now as He was going out on the road, one came running, knelt before Him, and asked Him, "Good Teacher, what shall I do that I may inherit eternal life?"*
> *So Jesus said to him, "Why do you call Me good? No one is good but One, that is, God. You know the commandments: 'Do not commit adultery,' 'Do not*

> *murder,' 'Do not steal,' 'Do not bear false witness,' 'Do not defraud,' 'Honor your father and your mother.' "*
>
> *And he answered and said to Him, "Teacher, all these things I have kept from my youth."*
>
> *Then Jesus, looking at him, loved him, and said to him, "One thing you lack: Go your way, sell whatever you have and give to the poor, and you will have treasure in heaven; and come, take up the cross, and follow Me."*
>
> *But he was sad at this word, and went away sorrowful, for he had great possessions.*
>
> MARK 10:17-22 NKJV

Money is not the root of all evil, but the love of it is (1 Timothy 6:10). What do you love more than Jesus? What promptings of His Spirit are you ignoring because you can't seem to give it up? Don't think your off the hook if it's family, not technically sin, or a so-called personality trait.

The bottom line is, your life is not your own. It's been bought with a high price. And ultimately you have to die, so that Christ's life can shine through yours. Otherwise, you will not be able to fully experience the life God created you to live.

Being a Living Sacrifice

Before the prodigal son journeyed home, his circumstances and wastefulness caused him to unintentionally "do without," so much so that he wanted to eat pig food (Luke 15:14-16). He was actually in a fasted state when he "came to his senses," and realized he wanted to return to the father (verse 17). I believe there is something we can get out of putting ourselves in a similar position.

In the midst of Jesus telling His disciples how to pray, how to not store up treasures on earth, and to seek first the kingdom of God, Jesus gives some instructions on fasting:

> *But when you fast, comb your hair and wash your face. Then no one will notice that you are fasting, except your Father, who knows what you do in private. And your Father, who sees everything, will reward you.*
>
> MATTHEW 6:17-18 NLT

Part of laying down your life often includes putting things aside for a time. Denying yourself food, helps your body know that it is not your boss, and that you are seeking the things of the spirit. As Jesus Himself fasted for 40 days and nights before beginning His earthly ministry, He said, "Man shall not live on bread alone, but on every word that comes out of the mouth of God (Matthew 4:4 NASB)."

I have been fasting breakfast in preparation to writing this. I plan to continue that as well as some other fasts, including times without any kind of food and certain types of media. I'm not telling you this to impress you, I really only want to receive the Father's reward. But I need to encourage you to also seek Him and see if there's any good thing you should abstain from for a time. The benefits of fasting are well worth the challenge. More importantly though, your actions will confirm that your life is not your own and you belong to God.

> *Beloved friends, what should be our proper response to God's marvelous mercies? To surrender yourselves to God to be his sacred, living sacrifices. And live in holiness, experiencing all that delights his heart. For this becomes your genuine expression of worship.*
>
> ROMANS 12:1 TPT

When Jesus told His followers so many times to take up their crosses, He was prophesying of His own cross. He was the lamb of God, destined from before the foundation of the earth to be a sacrifice. Not only did He live in perfect submission to His Father, He literally carried His cross up a hill, and on it shed His lifeblood, to wash away the sins of the world.

When Jesus looks in your eyes and says, "Take up your cross and follow me," remember nothing compares to what He has to offer you. I am not speaking about food anymore, but your whole life. As you lay everything on the altar, before Him, you will find true life. And He will be pleased with your living sacrifice.

Pray today:

> *Abba, like the prodigal son who suddenly realized his state, I am coming to my senses (Luke 15:14-21). The life I have been living is not the one that Jesus died for me to have. There are things that have carried me away captive. I have squandered your provision of grace, resources, favor, and time. I have tried to recover in my own strength, but I am at the end of my rope. I humble myself before you and repent.*

I am turning away from all this. I regret it. I am done saying rote prayers of asking for blanket forgiveness, knowing that my heart is still holding onto things that are not good for me. I lay it all down at your feet right now. I do not want to gain the world and lose my soul.

I recognize that there is more to this life than what is in the natural, and my choices have eternal consequences. I recognize that my lack of zeal, my dead fire, my dullness equates to time lost in the destiny that you have for me. And could even mean missed opportunities to lead others into a relationship with You.

I'm sorry for acting as if the things in my heart and my choices only effect me. I must admit, even my home is effected by what I have allowed in. So I am declaring that I want to change. I want to transform. I want freedom. I know that it comes by picking up my cross and following Jesus.

So this repentance is not just a temporary dropping of vices, but it is a complete reversal. I seek that my whole life would be turned around and set on the right course. I don't want to just stop and be broken down on the side of the road. I want to be restored and heading in the right direction, following Jesus, and living in the fullness of what You have to offer me. Thank You, Lord. Amen!

Journaling prompt:

Whatever is holding you back from following Jesus fully, and living the life He created you to live—needs to go. The word renunciation means disowning something and giving it up. And repentance involves a change of heart toward something else. Write down a declaration of your heart turning away from, and that you are giving up each thing that the Holy Spirit prompts you. We will talk more about this later, but you'll find it helpful to speak this repentance and renunciation out loud, and declare it any time you feel tempted to fall for the same trap again.

If you feel you are supposed to fast something, write down what you are giving up and the duration. It's good to know and have a plan. It can make it easier to fast food for longer durations if you ease into it by limiting more and more types of food over the span of a few days.

_____
_____
_____
_____
_____
_____
_____
_____
_____
_____
_____
_____
_____
_____
_____
_____

REKINDLING *the* FIRE

Day 3:

WILLING TO BE A SLAVE, BUT WITH A SON'S MINDSET

After washing their feet, He put his robe on and returned to His place at the table. "Do you understand what I just did?" Jesus said. "You've called me your teacher and Lord, and you're right, for that's who I am. So if I'm your teacher and Lord and have just washed your dirty feet, then you should follow the example that I've set for you and wash one another's dirty feet. Now do for each other what I have just done for you. I speak to you timeless truth: a servant is not superior to his master, and an apostle is never greater than the one who sent him. So now put into practice what I have done for you, and you will experience a life of happiness enriched with

> *untold blessings!"*
> John 13:12-17 TPT

AS THE PRODIGAL son decided to come home, he thought he would be a slave in his father's house. God has not given us a spirit of slavery, or bondage, as some translations say in Romans 8:15. This bondage connotes a tying up that isn't freely chosen, like enslavement to an addiction, or like human trafficking. But in the Hebrew culture being a slave, a bondservant, was often voluntary and had an end date (assuming the person did not choose to remain in that position).

Although we see the father quickly restore the prodigal son, he was genuinely willing to return as a slave. Likewise, we need to follow in the footsteps of Jesus, and submit ourselves to Abba, as a son who is also an obedient and thankful servant. We must utterly submit our will to Him, and show our love by doing what He says (John 14:15). Instead, we often ignore the nudges of the Father, His gentle correction, because we want to have control of our lives.

I believe part of what led to Jesus calling me a prodigal was that I assumed God was leading me when He wasn't anymore. When I entered a season of finding it hard to hear Him, I didn't press in enough and wait for direction. Then I made some consequential choices that I thought made sense based on God's previous leading. I figured He could correct me if I was wrong, but I began to remove myself from Abba's loving discipline, and I ignored His warnings. While He continued to graciously use me, the refining fire started to wane.

It's true, we can trust that we are led by the Holy Spirit as children of God. We need to mature to a place of being able to do the things we know the Father wants us to do, without needing to be constantly told. Jesus lived this way, but He also regularly went into solitude to meet with His Abba. We absolutely have to check in with the Father too, giving Him room to speak, receiving His direction, rebuke, and course correction. As well, we must allow the Holy Spirit within us to lead in the moment. We shouldn't ignore His wisdom, discernment, and gentle promptings.

A prince who quits serving his father shouldn't expect to continue receiving all the benefits of the kingdom. What's worse is if he starts to make choices opposed to the king's wishes, it will sow division and rebellion in his heart and the people he is leading. Likewise, when we make choices that aren't in line with God's purposes for us, and we try to get something apart from His will, we are falling into rebellion (which is as sinful as witchcraft 1 Samuel 15:23 NLT).

But when we remain bonded to God as a free act of our will, our life comes into order, and we can expect to receive the benefits of His heavenly kingdom. The Father's fire continues to purify and stoke our passions. We can choose to obey in hope and joy, trusting that He has our best interest at heart. It really comes down to relationship, and how we think about following Jesus in this life.

Mindset Changes Everything

It's important that we stay away from a slave mindset, of involuntary bondage that is actually demonic in it's roots. Always remember that God is thoroughly good (Mark 10:18). When He commands us, it's in love and for our good. He doesn't press-down, abuse, put in hard labor, and keep people bound up against their will. He gently leads, desiring our partnership, and that we would choose obedience out of love, faith, and devotion.

In this manner, Paul called himself a bondservant to God, recognizing his great indebtedness for salvation. And He was actually copying Jesus, a Son with complete access to the kingdom, yet humbly and willingly choosing to be a servant.

> ***Let this mind be in you which was also in Christ Jesus****, who, being in the form of God, did not consider it robbery to be equal with God, but made Himself of no reputation,* **taking the form of a bondservant***, and coming in the likeness of men. And being found in appearance as a man,* **He humbled Himself and became obedient to the point of death***, even the death of the cross. Therefore God also has highly exalted Him and given Him the name which is above every name, that at the name of Jesus every knee should bow, of those in heaven, and of those on earth, and of those under the earth, and that every tongue should confess that Jesus Christ is Lord, to the glory of God the Father.*
> PHILIPPIANS 2:5-11 NKJV
> (EMPHASIS ADDED)

Could we not only be willing to be a bondservant to our Heavenly Father, but even obedient to the point of death, like our Savior modeled for us? I think we could if we had His mindset, as this verse tells us to do. Jesus had no doubt about His Father's goodness, and for the joy set before Him endured the cross

(Hebrews 12:2). Having this faith, will help us to expect good things on the other side of hardship that comes through obedience.

> *"Therefore humble yourselves under the mighty hand of God [set aside self-righteous pride], so that He may exalt you [to a place of honor in His service] at the appropriate time, casting all your cares [all your anxieties, all your worries, and all your concerns, once and for all] on Him, for He cares about you [with deepest affection, and watches over you very carefully]."*
> 1 PETER 5:6-7 AMP (SEE ALSO JAMES 4:10)

Instead of trying to gain approval, wealth, and dignity in the eyes of the world we should seek God's kingdom and lay this life down. Submitting to the Holy Spirit in this way, proves we can be entrusted with much. This reward and responsibility can come partially in this life, but ultimately it is received in heaven.

> *For no one can lay a foundation other than the one which is laid, which is Jesus Christ. Now if anyone builds on the foundation with gold, silver, precious stones, wood, hay, or straw, each one's work will become evident; for the day will show it because it is to be revealed with fire, and the fire itself will test the quality of each one's work. If anyone's work which he has built on it remains, he will receive a reward. If anyone's work is burned up, he*

> *will suffer loss; but he himself will be saved, yet only so as through fire.*
> 1 CORINTHIANS 3:11-15 NASB
> (see also Matthew 5:12, Matthew 16:27, and 2 Timothy 4:8)

Jesus was raised up to the highest honor because of His incomprehensible obedience and sacrifice. As we humble ourselves now and invest in eternity, we will surely be raised up as well. We should allow our life to be refined, giving everything to the Father for Him to test with His fire. What we give up with the goal of serving the King, will never compare to what we will gain!

Pray today:

> *Father, I humbly come to you again and wholeheartedly bow down at your feet. You are my good King. I am your faithful bond-servant. The immense price You paid for this life will not allow me to waste it on my own carnal pleasures. I submit my time, resources, and affections to You. Thoroughly search me, and correct where there is anything not good for me, my family, or Your kingdom and purposes. Please refine everything with Your holy fire, and set me ablaze for You!*
>
> *I know that I represent You as a child, therefore I need to be careful that my heart, words, and actions bring You glory and honor. Please root out from me any ungodly fear, slave mentality of bondage, and any selfish pride,*

willfulness, rebellion, or witchcraft. Thank you, Jesus, for helping me to have Your mindset, that all of this would come from my identity as a child of God, and I would passionately operate out of faith, hope, and love. It's in Your name, Jesus, that I pray. Amen!

Journaling prompt:

Spend some time with your Abba, and ask Him to deal with any wrong mindsets or trust issues you are facing, as well as for Him to make any loving corrections to your life. Write down what He shows you and declare your desire to have the mind of Christ. Joyfully obey as His devoted child.

_____
_____
_____
_____
_____
_____
_____
_____
_____
_____
_____
_____
_____
_____
_____
_____
_____

Day 4:

Removing Previous Identities and Cleansing with Water

And such some of you were [once]. But you were washed clean (purified by a complete atonement for sin and made free from the guilt of sin), and you were consecrated (set apart, hallowed), and you were justified [pronounced righteous, by trusting] in the name of the Lord Jesus Christ and in the [Holy] Spirit of our God. Everything is permissible (allowable and lawful) for me; but not all things are helpful (good for me to do, expedient and profitable when considered with other things). Everything is lawful for me, but I

> *will not become the slave of anything or be brought under its power.*
>
> 1 CORINTHIANS 6:11-12 AMPC

WE TALKED ABOUT the right mindset of submitting to God and being willing to serve in yesterday's devotional. And we have dealt with our affections toward sin with some repentance and renunciation. But when coming to the Father, willing to be His bond-servant, we need to make sure of a few things. One that we are not continuing under a wrong identity, and secondly that we are not yoked to any other slave-master.

When we begin to practice sin or place other things above God, a part of our hearts comes under bondage to those things, and we become labeled as a practitioner of that sinful behavior. This is part of the reason that we feel a pulling back, a temptation to return to what we try to give up. A part of our identity has become wrapped up in it. Check out the verses immediately before the ones quoted at the beginning of this chapter.

> *Do you not know that the unrighteous will not inherit the kingdom of God? Do not be deceived. Neither fornicators, nor idolaters, nor adulterers, nor homosexuals, nor sodomites, nor thieves, nor covetous, nor drunkards, nor revilers, nor extortioners will inherit the kingdom of God.*
>
> 1 CORINTHIANS 6:9-10 NKJV

This is not an exhaustive list of types of sinners, but it's a great start, and helps illustrate my point. All of these are identities. A fornicator practices sexual sin. This is what he or she does. It has become a part of their character, and they have become titled as such.

Thankfully, it also says, "such some of you *were*... (verse 11)," meaning these labels can be removed. Let me put it this way, I continued to struggle with temptation to drink while I still carried the nature of an alcoholic. When I really got rid of that identity, I became much stronger in refusing the temptations that the enemy continued trying to trap me with.

Paul goes on to say that even practices that are allowed, can ensnare us and make us slaves. This goes back to the idea that the love of a good thing, upon exceeding the love we have for Christ, means we need to lay it down as a sacrifice. We will talk tomorrow about further freedom from slave-masters, as I want to give plenty of time to focus on the identity aspect today.

Casting Off Former Identities

Jesus stopped and said, "Call him here." So they went to the blind man and said, "Have courage! Get up! Jesus is calling for you!" So he threw off his beggars' cloak, jumped up, and made his way to Jesus.

Jesus said to him, "What do you want me to do for you?"

The man replied, "My Master, please, let me see again!"

Jesus responded, "Your faith heals you. Go in peace, with your sight restored." All at once, the man's eyes opened and he could see again, and he began at once to follow Jesus, walking down the

road with him.
MARK 10:49-52 TPT

When Jesus called this man who was blind to Him, he cast off his outer garment that designated him as a beggar. His status as a blind man allowed for him to ask for money. And in that time and culture, they wore garments showing this. I believe his faith was so strong, that he knew he would not need that label anymore.

Like this man, we must know that Jesus will heal us, and we will walk with our Savior in a new life. We also have to throw away the things that identify us as anything other than a follower of Jesus (even literal physical objects often). At the same time as being willing to serve God, we have to get rid of our likeness and mindset of a slave to another. We have to be a son, with all the benefits of sonship, who is willing to serve the Father rather than our previous slave-owners.

When the prodigal son humbly approached the father, genuinely ready to be a slave, he was wearing the dirty garments of a pig feeder. Can you imagine if he continued to wear those clothes at the feast his father prepared? A special robe was given him, and I guarantee that he didn't just put it on top of his old clothing. He needed to be washed clean of that label, so he could return to the position his father had for him.

Putting On Christ

Once we have taken off these old ways, we need to actually stop calling ourselves whatever we used to be before. Not only that but we must change the way we think, speak, and act. More powerful than only abstaining from these ways of living, is replacing them with God's ways.

> *"For you are all children of God through faith in Christ Jesus. And all who have been united with Christ in baptism have put on Christ, like putting on new clothes."*
>
> GALATIANS 3:26-27 NLT (SEE ALSO COLOSSIANS 3:1-17)

The Father wants to wash you clean of the guilt of sin. He has set you apart for Him. He has pronounced you as righteous, by the precious blood of His beloved Son. This right standing with God is not because you have made yourself perfect, but because you have put on Christ. So you must strip yourself of all other identities, and live out the one He has graciously given you.

Pray today:

> *God, thank You that You have provided a way for every bondage to be removed, and for me to be cleansed by Your living water, and the blood of the Lamb. I cast off every ungodly garment that has labeled me and kept me in slavery to others. I want to be washed as clean as pure white snow and clothed in Christ. I want to be delivered from every corrupted mindset and belief, and anything else that would hold me back from walking in the identity You have for me as a son.*
>
> *I submit to Jesus every part of my character, every habit, and each pattern of thinking, declaring they have to be obedient to Christ. And every ungodly distraction and worldly or carnal way of living in me I lay on the altar. I ask You Lord to transform me, that I would not be*

brainwashed by this world, but that my mind and ways would be cleansed by living water, the blood of Christ, and anointed with the oil of the Spirit. I put on the mind of Christ and the helmet of salvation, along with the rest of the armor of God. I declare and decree that I am of a single mind and purpose, giving undivided attention to God and His kingdom. In Jesus's name, amen!

Journaling prompt:

Write down any identities you have carried that are not of God. Declare that you are removing the garments labeling you in this way, casting them at Jesus's feet. You may also need to get rid of physical objects, whether related to an addiction or the occult, etc. Ask Him to give you wisdom and discernment, bring healing, purify your heart, give you clean hands, and help you think and act in His ways.

Once you have done this, know that you have been truly washed clean and you have put on a new identity, which is Christ! So watch your thoughts, words, and actions. Stop declaring that you are a "_____" (whatever you were before that you are not now). If you notice you are thinking, speaking, or acting like you once did, immediately repent and declare that you have cast that off and you now walk in the character of the Son.

Even if you are getting rid of a strong addiction, trust me, you will see change if you continue and don't give up. Tomorrow we will go even deeper to receive greater freedom and strength to overcome.

_____
_____

Rekindling *the* Fire

Day 5:

ONLY ONE MASTER

*No one can serve two masters;
for either he will hate the one and love the other,
or he will be devoted to one and despise the other*

MATTHEW 6:24 NASB

SOMETIMES WE CAN be in bondage to something and not know it. When this is the case, even as we genuinely desire to serve God, we will struggle to have wholehearted devotion. This is because there is a hidden mixture in us. While we may be following Jesus, and sealed with His Spirit for the day of redemption, we may also be unknowingly operating under another spirit than God's.

I limped along as a born-again believer, struggling with sin, bound to other slave-masters for nearly twenty years before I realized I could fight back. The fact of the matter is that we are in a war. The evil spirits mentioned in the Bible are real. They continue to deceive and manipulate today, but with God's help we can be free of them. (Some Bible passages are listed for reference at the end of today's devotional.)

I have experienced and seen real manifestations of demons,

and the casting of them out, in myself and many others I personally know. They don't just leave when we add the tag "Christian" to all the other labels we have carried. The good news is that liberty is attainable and makes way for deeper consecration to God. But we have to actively fight against them, commanding them to go in the name of Jesus, being filled with His Spirit, and replacing their ways with His.

Often a large level of deliverance happens at the same time as the salvation experience of giving your life to Jesus. But I am not aware of anyone who completely stopped sinning in all the ways that they acted out before. These areas are strongholds, not only in our minds, but also in our hearts and souls. They must be recognized and overtaken with the help of the Holy Spirit.

Strongholds Recovered for the King

Luke 11 is an amazing chapter that begins with Jesus teaching His disciples about prayer and then deliverance. He starts with how to seek the Father, how to persevere in faith, and how to believe that He will give you good things:

> *"What father among you, if his son asks for a fish, will give him a snake instead of a fish? Or if he asks for an egg, will give him a scorpion? If you, then, being evil [that is, sinful by nature], know how to give good gifts to your children, how much more will your heavenly Father give the Holy Spirit to those who ask and continue to ask Him!"*
> LUKE 11:11-13 AMP

I used to be confused by these verses in the context of the

preceding ones, thinking it random that Jesus suddenly brings in the Holy Spirit. They actually make more sense if you consider His illustration of a snake or a scorpion representing evil spirits. He undeniably referred to them this way in the previous chapter (Luke 10:17-20). He knew He was about to heal a man by casting out a mute spirit, and the religious rulers would say He did it by the power of the enemy.

So He was not only speaking of how we can ask and receive good things from the Father. Amazingly, He was also speaking in advance to the upcoming accusation. He says that His Father will not give you an evil spirit, but as the giver of good gifts, will give you His Holy Spirit. After explaining how it's ridiculous to think He would expel demons by their own power, Jesus goes on to say:

> *"But if I cast out demons with the finger of God, surely the kingdom of God has come upon you. When a strong man, fully armed, guards his own palace, his goods are in peace. But when a stronger than he comes upon him and overcomes him, he takes from him all his armor in which he trusted, and divides his spoils.*
> LUKE 11:20-22 NKJV

The strong man mentioned here is an evil spirit that has setup a stronghold in a person's life. But the stronger spirit that Jesus speaks of is the Holy Spirit. This is why the Holy Spirit needs to be involved in the work of deliverance, and He must fill the void of the spirits who were kicked out. Sadly, even when we truly experience deliverance, we can allow the demons to return by not giving the place over to the Holy Spirit, and/or by going back into slavery with our decisions.

> *"When an evil spirit leaves a person, it goes into the desert, searching for rest. But when it finds none, it says, 'I will return to the person I came from.' So it returns and finds that its former home is all swept and in order. Then the spirit finds seven other spirits more evil than itself, and they all enter the person and live there. And so that person is worse off than before."*
>
> LUKE 11:24-26 NLT

For you to remove the bonds of other slave-masters and be freed from their strongholds, God's kingdom must overcome and literally rule over that area of your heart. The answer is not perfect behavior in your own strength, but rather a humble accounting of what is going on, and a genuine desire to consecrate everything to the Holy Spirit.

Pray today:

> *Father God in Heaven, if I am a slave at all, let me be a bond-servant only to You, my good and loving King of kings. I do not want to be in bondage to any other masters. Please overwhelm these strongholds in my heart with Your Kingdom and Spirit. I repent of every ungodly allegiance and ask You, Jesus, to cleanse me and set me free by Your precious blood. Thank You for the identity You've given me, including authority in Your powerful name.*

Now, I stand in this authority over every demonic stronghold of slavery in my life, in the name of Jesus. Once again, I put on the whole armor of God and lift up the shield of faith against every fiery dart of the wicked one. I take the sword of the spirit and sever myself from the evil spirits attached to the bondages I have been under. I cut off every addiction to things that are not of God, along with all their deceptions, manipulations and temptations. I command them all to be gone from me right now in the name of Jesus Christ of Nazareth. I bind in chains and fetters of iron any remaining spirits who are not of God, and cast them out of my life right now, in Jesus's name!

I invite you, Jesus, to pour out Your Spirit and fill me to overflowing. Fill every place the enemy had, and take over their strongholds. Cleanse me with Your blood and living water, purify me with Your Holy fire, and fill me with Your glorious presence. Please help me to recognize when the enemy is trying to return, and help me to not fall for their temptations and give them access. Let these places become a strong tower of your Kingdom in my life, a testimony to others of the goodness and power of God, and a blessing to me, my family, and those around me. In Jesus's mighty name I pray, amen!

Journaling prompt:

It's good to pray in general, but we can't then assume it is all taken care of. Evil spirits will do anything they can to hold on, and you often have to recognize them and speak directly to each specific issue and every demon that is attached to it. In this journaling area write down the issues you are facing which could have demonic roots. After this, speak out loud with your words repent and plead the blood of Christ over yourself in regards to the issue. Then address the surrounding spirits specifically, calling them by the name of the issue or "every demon at work around" this issue. Take a firm stance and fiercely command them to go, out loud, in the name of Jesus. You should feel a change.

Continue to do this no matter how often the temptation returns or you continue to struggle. It will be a process of maturing, receiving discernment, recognizing where you need more freedom, and continuing to fight for it. This practice can also help if you sense demonic activity trying to affect your life and relationships.

The Greek word for spirit used in the Bible can be translated as breath or wind. I have seen in many deliverance sessions that spirits leave at the same time as coughing, sneezing, yawning, vomiting, etc. You do not need to make this happen, just note that you are probably getting freedom if you experience some of these things. Always remember to ask Jesus to seal the work of deliverance in His blood and Spirit, and that He would fill you again to overflowing with the Holy Spirit. Seek assistance from a trusted Christian inner healing and deliverance ministry if you need more help.

We'll talk more about the Holy Spirit later, but if you would like more information on being filled with the Holy Spirit, you can download this free PDF called Navigating the Maze of Life with God... As His Child, Filled with His Spirit, and Using His Gifts to Heal the World. This PDF is combined with other free material mentioned in the Introduction.

GodAndYouAndMe.com/Rekindling-Fire-Free-Stuff

This devotional is not meant to be a teaching material about spiritual beings. But to make sure you are aware that this subject is Biblical, here is a sprinkling of scripture passages from Genesis to Revelation, that refer to demonic and fallen angelic activity (not a comprehensive list):

- Genesis 3:1-19, 6:1-13
- Leviticus 17:7
- Deuteronomy 12:29-31
- 1 Samuel 16:14-23, 18:10-12
- Job 1:6-2:10
- Psalm 106:34-48
- Ezekiel 28:11-19
- Mark 1:34, 6:7-13
- Luke 8:26-39, 10:17-20
- Romans 1:22-25
- Ephesians 2:1-2, 3:8-12, 6:10-18
- 2 Corinthians 4:4, 10:3-6
- 1 John 5:19

Rekindling the Fire

- Revelation 12:9

Day 6:

THE WARFARE OF CAPTURING THOUGHTS AND TEARING DOWN STRONGHOLDS

For though we walk (live) in the flesh, we are not carrying on our warfare according to the flesh and using mere human weapons.
For the weapons of our warfare are not physical [weapons of flesh and blood], but they are mighty before God for the overthrow and destruction of strongholds,
[Inasmuch as we] refute arguments and theories and reasonings and every proud and lofty thing that sets itself up against the [true] knowledge of God; and we lead every thought and purpose away

> *captive into the obedience of Christ (the Messiah, the Anointed One)*
>
> 2 CORINTHIANS 10:3-5 AMPC

THE APOSTLE PAUL was not only being eloquent and quotable while writing the above passage. He meant for us to actually do this. I had read and heard these verses many times before I ever tried to practically apply them. For years I was asleep during this spiritual war, and I was being plundered by the enemy.

When I realized that I was not powerless over the things going on in my head, but that I could actually take my thoughts captive and force them to obey Jesus—everything changed. We may not recognize their voices, but temptation, fear, greed, rage, doubt, selfish ambition, pride, anxiety, rebellion, etc., are actually shouting that something is bigger than our God. According to the verses above, we are able to transform our hearts and minds, and tear down the enemy's strongholds.

Spiritual Warfare—Tearing Down Strongholds

The war that we are waging is not a physical one, and our weapons are not weak:

> *For we do not wrestle against flesh and blood, but against principalities, against powers, against the rulers of the darkness of this age, against spiritual hosts of wickedness in the heavenly places. Therefore take up the whole armor of God, that you may be able to withstand in the evil day, and*

having done all, to stand.

Stand therefore, having girded your waist with truth, having put on the breastplate of righteousness, and having shod your feet with the preparation of the gospel of peace; above all, taking the shield of faith with which you will be able to quench all the fiery darts of the wicked one. And take the helmet of salvation, and the sword of the Spirit, which is the word of God; praying always with all prayer and supplication in the Spirit, being watchful to this end with all perseverance and supplication for all the saints

EPHESIANS 6:12-18 NKJV

Based on what we read yesterday, we know there are evil spirits. Even after they have been exposed and kicked out, according to Jesus's words in Luke 11:24-26, they will try to return. The thing is, most Christians don't recognize them, because they hide themselves in our thoughts and emotions.

How to recognize an evil spirit? Perhaps a temptation that continues to come back, an ungodly thought that returns over and over, or a persistent harmful emotion that seems to take over. We usually feel helpless, as if we have no control over these things. Instead of addressing the evil spirits at work behind them, we run to doctors, counselors, and our false comforters.

I am not saying that we can't get help from others, but many people never address the dark spiritual element. We may beg God, but we often do not follow what scripture has told us to do. Though some will feel discouraged, overwhelmed, maybe even angry by the responsibility being placed on them, this is actually good news.

It means that you have been empowered to overcome. I say this as one who thought I would always struggle with alcohol, pornography, and video game addiction. One who would always have a hopeless feeling first thing in the morning. One who would struggle with rejection, a need to be understood, and thoughts of suicide for the rest of my life.

Although it was a hard war, consisting of many battles often mere seconds apart, I overcame these things by taking every thought captive. It seemed an impossible task at first, but eventually I became stronger and the enemy's foothold weaker. His attacks became fewer and farther between, and now I am able to recognize much quicker when he comes again. With the help of the Holy Spirit and His refining fire, all these strongholds were destroyed.

The Thief Must Pay Back Seven-Fold

Jesus refers to the enemy as the thief in John 10:10, saying, "The thief comes only to steal and kill and destroy; I came so that they would have life, and have it abundantly (NASB)." Besides trying to kill you and destroy your life, relationships, and property, the thief will take spoils. But thankfully we read yesterday that the Holy Spirit divides the strong man's spoils upon overcoming him (Luke 10:20-22).

> *Excuses might be found for a thief who steals because he is starving. But if he is caught, he must pay back seven times what he stole, even if he has to sell everything in his house.*
>
> PROVERBS 6:30-31 NLT

When you capture the thief with the help of the Holy Spirit, you are entitled to be repaid. In other words, the things that the enemy has illegally done to steal and kill and destroy in your life—God wants to restore—even seven-fold!

Don't take for granted that this will automatically happen. You must claim this promise! Declare that the enemy has been caught and must repay even to the point of losing everything he has.

Jesus came to give you life, and life abundantly. We'll talk tomorrow about the next step in preparing to receive this abundance. The key is submitting more and more of your body, soul, and spirit to Jesus. This puts you in a better position to receive His prosperity in every area!

Pray today:

King of glory, You are the Lord who is strong and mighty in battle (Psalm 24:8)! Thank You that as You have commanded me to put on the armor of God, You also have put on righteousness, salvation, vengeance, and zeal, and You repay my adversaries with wrath and retribution (Isaiah 59:15-20). Thank You that greater are You in me, Holy Spirit, than the strong man that is in the world (1 John 4:1-6). Thank You that You overcome his work in my life. That with Your help I am tearing down his strongholds, and this thief must repay seven-fold what he has stolen.

Please help me to recognize when these evil spirits are trying to return, take captive every thought, and force

> *them to be obedient to You, Jesus. I don't want to only know about this, but also to put it into practice. Thank You that You train my hands for war and my fingers for battle (Psalm 144:1), and that You help me to take up my spiritual armor and weaponry daily and stand against the evil one. I submit all of this to You, as well as every area of my body, soul, and spirit. In Jesus's name, I pray. Amen!*

Journaling prompt:

Write down any thoughts, feelings, struggles, ungodly personality traits, etc., that you have often struggled with. Submit them to God, and ask Him to help you think and feel the truth from His perspective. Each time you recognize that those thoughts and feelings are arising, submit them to God, and command them to obey Jesus, in your own heart. It may be helpful to also speak out loud against them and treat them in a similar way as an evil spirit if you feel the need. Also speaking and acting in an opposite spirit can be good, if it's appropriate. In other words, if you are struggling with selfishness or greed, going out of your way to help others and be generous will aid in your transformation.

It's not uncommon that these ungodly thoughts and feelings will try overwhelming you with a constant barrage, one after another in rapid succession, seemingly without end. Don't stop submitting them to God, even if you have to every second. I can attest that even in this situation, you can overcome them with the help of the Holy Spirit, consistency, and self-discipline. Give God praise and glory as you recognize that you are getting stronger and the work of the enemy is diminishing in your life!

REKINDLING *the* FIRE

Day 7:

Preparing the Soul to Receive

Bless the Lord, O my soul; And all that is within me, bless His holy name! Bless the Lord, O my soul, And forget not all His benefits: Who forgives all your iniquities, Who heals all your diseases, Who redeems your life from destruction, Who crowns you with lovingkindness and tender mercies, Who satisfies your mouth with good things, So that your youth is renewed like the eagle's.

Psalm 103:1-5 NKJV

THE WRONG IDENTITIES and wrong ideologies, that we have been talking about, have not only harmed our relationship with God and kept us from walking in a greater fulfillment of our destinies—they have damaged our souls and even our bodies. Where we have believed lies, where we have held on to doubt and unbelief, where we have harbored hopelessness, it has caused us to not receive all that God has for our bodies, souls, and spirits. We must return to a baseline of our souls blessing the Lord and forgetting none of His benefits.

All that's Within Me, Bless His Holy Name

In the period between David's anointing and actually becoming king, he suffered many hardships, but continued to trust the Lord. Here's one example:

> *So David and his men came to the town, and behold, it was burned, and their wives and sons and daughters were taken captive.*
> *Then David and the men with him lifted up their voices and wept until they had no more strength to weep...*
> *David was greatly distressed, for the men spoke of stoning him because the souls of them all were bitterly grieved, each man for his sons and daughters. But David encouraged and strengthened himself in the Lord his God.*
> 1 SAMUEL 30:3-4, 6 AMPC

Too often we stay under the reality of our storm clouds, forgetting that the Sun is still shining in a blue sky above it all. Even when it appeared everything was lost, David encouraged and strengthened himself in God. He knew that the Lord was greater than his greatest trial. But he needed to remind his soul and his situation of that fact. He ended up seeking the Lord for direction, and God helped him recover all that was lost in this situation.

Psalm 103 is attributed also to David, and in its words we see his habit of commanding his soul to bless God and remember His goodness. Whether we are suffering because of the fallen nature of this world, because of spiritual attacks, or because of our own mistakes—we must also speak to ourselves, defying our circumstances, and reminding everything within us to bless His Holy Name.

Forget Not All His Benefits

Although we, like the prodigal son, have put ourselves in positions that led to brokenness, as we return to our Abba Father, He surprisingly shows us kindness and help. What do you need? According to the devotional's opening Bible passage, God:

- forgives all your iniquities
- heals all your diseases
- redeems your life from destruction
- crowns you with lovingkindness and tender mercies
- satisfies your mouth with good things
- renews your youth like the eagle's

Where I and my family serve as missionaries, the Italians have a saying, "Tra il dire e il fare, c'è di mezzo il mare," which translates as, "Between saying and doing, there is the sea." We can be thankful that God's Word is true, it doesn't return void, and in Christ, His promises are yes (Numbers 23:19, Isaiah 55:11, 2 Corinthians 1:20). However, unlike God, I can know and say something, but have a lot of trouble doing it.

My problem with the benefits of God are not a lack of

knowledge, but a lack of practically believing and receiving. Even to move beyond the idea that He has forgiven all my iniquities is sometimes a struggle. In these last twenty years of following Jesus (and looking back to the first half of my life as well), He has proven faithful over and over. So I must remind myself of His benefits, believe that they are for me, bring my needs to Him, and thank and praise Him in advance of His promises coming to fruition.

> *Beloved, I pray that in all respects you may prosper and be in good health, just as your soul prospers.*
> 3 JOHN 1:2 NASB

It is God's will for you to prosper in all respects. The bottleneck between His benefits and your life just might be your soul. Whatever you are going through, command your soul to bless the Lord, and it will prosper. Then as you look at your circumstances, remember all of God's benefits, apply the promise of His Word to what you need, and praise Him even before your breakthrough.

Our Hearts are Like Gardens Waiting for Cultivation

We have been doing a lot this week to receive from our Abba. It has been hard work of digging deep, and removing the things that will keep us from reaping a bountiful reward. Jesus likened our hearts to fields where the seed of God's Word is being sown (Mark 4:1-20). The Father has planned a beautiful garden that will yield fruit which blesses us and those around us.

> *How beautiful are your tents, O Jacob;*
> *how lovely are your homes, O Israel!*
> *They spread before me like palm groves,*
> *like gardens by the riverside.*
> *They are like tall trees planted by the Lord,*
> *like cedars beside the waters.*
> NUMBERS 24:5-6 NLT

He wants our hearts to be a place of communion with Him. But according to Jesus's parable of the Sower in Mark 4:1-20, there are many things that can hinder cultivation. Though this week may not have been the most fun times of devotion, we have been preparing ourselves to enter in to Abba's festival celebration.

In order for His Word to go deep, we have been:

- scattering the birds that would eat the seed, representing the enemy and what is coming against us
- tilling the soil and removing hardness, through repentance and humility, so the seed can go deep
- pulling up the weeds that would choke out the seed's growth, by removing wrong mindsets and the things that steal our affections.

> "But what is sown on good soil represents those who open their hearts to receive the message and their lives bear good fruit—some yield a harvest of thirty, sixty, even a hundredfold!"
> MARK 4:20 TPT

By doing this work, you are opening yourself to receive and bear good fruit. This courtyard of your heart is ready for the King to design. No human could plan the magnificent place He will make for you to meet with Him. God is transforming your heart beyond your imagination and ability. Because you are His child, and He loves you with an everlasting love.

Pray today:

Abba, I come to You, desiring to bless You and recognize Your goodness. I submit my soul, all my thoughts, desires, and emotions, to You. And in the mighty name of Jesus, I command my soul, and everything that is within me, to bless Your holy name. I speak to my soul to remember the good things You have done, and believe what Your Word says You will do.

Thank You for forgiving all my iniquities, healing all my diseases, redeeming my life from destruction, crowning me with lovingkindness and tender mercies, satisfying my mouth with good things, and renewing my youth like the eagle's. I receive all these blessings in faith, believing that You are a rewarder of those who diligently seek You (Hebrews 11:6).

For every trial I am going through, and every brokenness within me—no matter how long I have suffered them—I receive Your benefits. As I bless You, please help my soul to prosper. May my life also prosper and be in good health, in all respects. Please design a beautiful place in my heart—not only for the work of bearing fruit, but

also where I can commune with You. Thank You, Jesus.
I pray all of this in Your holy name. Amen!

Journaling prompt:

In regards to the areas you are struggling, consider each of the benefits listed in Psalm 103:1-5 (as well as any others you remember from scripture). Pray and journal how You believe God is faithful and will help you. Ask Him to continue working on your heart, that it would be His to design, and that you can meet with Him there.

_____
_____
_____
_____
_____
_____
_____
_____
_____
_____
_____
_____
_____
_____
_____
_____
_____
_____
_____

REKINDLING *the* FIRE

Congratulations on completing the first seven days of this twenty-one-day devotional!

This is just the beginning, but it has restored the foundation needed to rekindle the fire. I am not only writing these for you, but also receiving and practicing each subject again for myself. I recommend not rushing through these daily devotionals, but rather allowing the Father to sow each seed deeply. I hope you will take more time where needed and do your part to facilitate the growth and bearing of fruit that remains (John 15:16).

In the 2nd week we will seek restoration of our identity as children of God. We'll focus on Luke 15:22 when the Father says, "Quickly bring out the best robe [for the guest of honor] and put it on him; and give him a ring for his hand, and sandals for his feet (AMP)." And continue to build ourselves up with the following topics:

- Restoring the Secret Meeting Place with God
- Being Anointed and Receiving Healing
- Hosting the Presence of God
- Rekindling the Fire
- Putting on Salvation, Righteousness, and Celebration
- Keys to Worshiping in Spirit and Truth
- Standing Restored as a Joint-Heir with Christ

Then in the last week we will go deeper into our calling of following in Jesus's footsteps, reflecting His glory, and living in the destiny of who God created us to be!

Day 8:

Meeting with the King in the Secret Place

*He who dwells in the secret place of the
Most High shall remain stable and
fixed under the shadow of the Almighty
[Whose power no foe can withstand].
I will say of the Lord, He is my Refuge and
my Fortress, my God; on Him I lean and rely,
and in Him I [confidently] trust!
For [then] He will deliver you from the snare of
the fowler and from the deadly pestilence.
[Then] He will cover you with His pinions, and
under His wings shall you trust and find refuge;
His truth and His faithfulness
are a shield and a buckler.*

PSALM 91:1-4 AMPC

ALTHOUGH I CONTINUED to pray and sporadically give God undivided attention, I fell out of the practice of habitually meeting Him in the secret place. If you're in this position too, you must return to regular times of devotion again. This is a mark of being a child of your heavenly Father, as Jesus regularly went into secluded places to seek His Abba (Luke 5:16).

We need to heed what Jesus taught His disciples when He said, "But when you pray, go away by yourself, shut the door behind you, and pray to your Father in private. Then your Father, who sees everything, will reward you (Matthew 6:6 NLT)." King David had learned this also, and wrote these powerful words:

O God, You are my God; Early will I seek You;
My soul thirsts for You; My flesh longs for You
In a dry and thirsty land Where there is no water.
So I have looked for You in the sanctuary,
To see Your power and Your glory.
Because Your lovingkindness is better than life,
My lips shall praise You.
Thus I will bless You while I live;
I will lift up my hands in Your name.
My soul shall be satisfied
as with marrow and fatness,
And my mouth shall praise You with joyful lips.
When I remember You on my bed,
I meditate on You in the night watches.
Because You have been my help,
Therefore in the shadow of Your wings
I will rejoice.

> *My soul follows close behind You;*
> *Your right hand upholds me.*
> PSALM 63:1-8 NKJV

Entering in By the Blood of the Lamb

It was costly for the Father to make a way for us to enter into His presence. He is holy, and apart from Jesus's work on the cross, we are not. God was willing for the precious blood of His only begotten Son to be shed, because He so wanted to restore our relationship with Him.

> *Let's approach the throne of grace with confidence, so that we may receive mercy and find grace for help at the time of our need.*
> *... we have confidence to enter the holy place by the blood of Jesus, by a new and living way which He inaugurated for us through the veil, that is, through His flesh, and since we have a great priest over the house of God, let's approach God with a sincere heart in full assurance of faith, having our hearts sprinkled clean from an evil conscience and our bodies washed with pure water.*
> HEBREWS 4:16, 10:19-20 NASB

As we enter into this throne-room, this holy place, this time of seeking Him in the stillness—we can rest in His presence and receive what we need from our Abba. Sometimes this will be in the form of a dialog between you and God. Sometimes it can look like you bowing, sitting, or laying still, quieting your thoughts, and waiting until He speaks or shows you something. Sometimes you will read the Bible and allow the Holy Spirit to teach you.

Later in this week's devotional we'll look into a couple of these things, and remember how vital they are to living the life God created us to live. But for now, let's focus purely on prioritizing time with our heavenly Father.

Valuing Time with the King

When we have ignored the promptings of the Holy Spirit and our Abba's still small voice, not only have we allowed the influence of the enemy, but we have also broken trust. Father God graciously and mercifully restores us quickly, but He is a person, and relationships take time to heal. He will always be faithful, so we too should strive for faithfulness and prove our intentions over time. We must show God that we value Him!

> *"The Kingdom of Heaven is like a treasure that a man discovered hidden in a field. In his excitement, he hid it again and sold everything he owned to get enough money to buy the field."*
> MATTHEW 13:44 NLT

What price would you pay to have unlimited access to the King of kings and the lover of your soul? Jesus paid this incomprehensible cost. How could we ever take this for granted and let our passions grow cold? He is warming your heart and bidding you draw near to His throne of grace—today, and every day.

Stirring Up Your Passion

The true yearnings of our hearts are revealed in how we spend our time. I am not saying this to bring guilt and condemnation, but so we can evaluate where priorities need to shift. When a person is in love, no one needs to tell them to prioritize their loved one. This is how we want to be with God, so we must stoke that first love fire (Revelation 2:4-5).

One of the most powerful helpers for falling in love with God is knowing Him more. Not necessarily theologically, but relationally—like the seasoned husband and wife know one another. Continuing to read His Word and receive what He wants to reveal in the secret place will increase your relational knowledge of Him, and thereby increase your passion. These also happen to be keys to worshiping in spirit and truth, which we will talk about later this week.

When you begin (or begin again) coming to your place of prayer and meeting with God, it might be a sheer effort of discipline. But as you faithfully continue investing in your relationship with Him, this labor turns into excitement and joy. As you receive His revelation and know Him more, your passion and love will increase. He sees the deepest places of your heart, knowing where you genuinely appreciate and desire Him. And where you still need transformation, He will pour out His fiery love which refines.

> *Then you will call upon Me and go and pray to Me, and I will listen to you. And you will seek Me and find Me, when you search for Me with all your heart.*
> JEREMIAH 29:12-13 NKJV

Pray today:

King of kings, thank You for the price You paid to meet with me. Thank You for making a way for me to enter into Your holy place and the throne-room of grace, by the precious blood of Your Son, Jesus. Thank You, Abba, for doing this because you desire me to come to you in relationship. Please forgive me for my inconsistency and taking the fact that You would meet with me for granted. Please forgive me for all the times that You have waited on me and I didn't show up. Please restore our relationship, and help me to be faithful and consistent.

I honor You, and recognize that meeting with You is the best part of my day. You are my greatest priority, and if I get nothing else done, at least I will have accomplished something that has eternal value—investing in our relationship! I know that this investment and discipline, will stir up my passion for You and turn into my greatest joy. I pray that You would help me to seek You and find You, and fall in love with You more and more. In Jesus's name, amen!

Journaling prompt:

Pray and journal to God about how you value Him and want to meet with Him. Write to Him a time and place that you would like to meet Him consistently. If possible, make this a quiet, secluded place where you can seek Him without distractions. Sometimes life makes it hard to do this, but even if it's impossible to have an isolated place with a lot of time to spend with Jesus, make sure you are valuing Him by seeking Him daily.

If you once spent time with God regularly, but have stopped, repent for what has gotten between You and Him. The prodigal son left the Father, but then he realized his mistake and returned. I am speaking from this place. What could ever make me forget the value of meeting with Him?

Rekindling *the* Fire

Day 9:

ANOINTED FOR CONSECRATION

Beautiful words stir my heart.
I will recite a lovely poem about the King,
for my tongue is like the pen of a skillful poet.
You are the most handsome of all.
Gracious words stream from Your lips.
God himself has blessed You forever.
Put on Your sword, O mighty warrior!
You are so glorious, so majestic!
In Your majesty, ride out to victory,
defending truth, humility, and justice.
Go forth to perform awe-inspiring deeds!
Your arrows are sharp, piercing Your enemies'
hearts. The nations fall beneath Your feet.
Your throne, O God, endures forever and ever.
You rule with a scepter of justice.
You love justice and hate evil.
Therefore God, Your God, has anointed You,
pouring out the oil of joy on You

> *more than on anyone else.*
> ***Myrrh, aloes, and cassia perfume Your robes.***
> *In ivory palaces the music of strings*
> *entertains You.*
> *Kings' daughters are among Your noble women.*
> *At Your right side stands the queen,*
> *wearing jewelry of finest gold from Ophir!*
> *Listen to me, O royal daughter;*
> *take to heart what I say.*
> *Forget your people and your family far away.*
> *For your royal husband delights in your beauty;*
> *honor him, for He is your Lord."*
>
> PSALMS 45:1-11 NLT
> (EMPHASIS ADDED)

JESUS IS THE most awesome and majestic Warrior-King. Although we are lowly compared to Him, He lifts us up. He is the only begotten Son of God, and yet He is the firstborn of many brethren. While He was anointed with the oil of gladness above all His siblings, Abba desires to anoint us as well.

When we come humbly in our filthy rags, covered in miry clay, the Father will say to His servants, "Bring out the best robe and put it on him, and put a ring on his hand and sandals on his feet (Luke 15:22 NKJV)."

We mentioned this also in Day 4, when we talked about removing previous identities and being cleansed with water. Before donning this fine clothing from his father, the prodigal son surely removed his old garments and washed himself. But he was also likely anointed with rich and fragrant oils.

Can you imagine how undeserving and blessed he must have felt? He is only asking to be placed among the servants, and he is treated like a prince! In this same way, we are, as we return wholeheartedly to the King of kings, our Heavenly Father. Psalm 23:5 in The Passion Translation notes that oil is a representation of the Holy Spirit and so it reads, "You anoint me with the fragrance of Your Holy Spirit; You give me all I can drink of You until my cup overflows."

The Anointing Is a Setting Apart for God

In the book of Exodus, God instructed Moses on how to make a special anointing oil. He was told to use it to set apart for God the tent of meeting, the tabernacle furnishings, and the priests:

"You shall also consecrate them,
that they may be most holy;
whatever touches them shall be holy.
You shall anoint Aaron and his sons,
and consecrate them,
that they may minister as priests to Me.
You shall speak to the sons of Israel, saying,
'This shall be a holy anointing oil to Me
throughout your generations."

EXODUS 30:29-31 NASB

Later the Lord called the High Priest Samuel to anoint the first Israelite king named Saul, and God's Spirit came upon him. But when Saul didn't follow God's instructions, Samuel was told to anoint another king:

> *Then Samuel took the horn of oil and anointed him in the midst of his brothers; and the Spirit of the Lord came upon David from that day forward...*
> *But the Spirit of the Lord departed from Saul, and a distressing spirit from the Lord troubled him.*
> 1 SAMUEL 16:13-14 NKJV

These objects and people were set apart for God, meaning they were separated from ungodly use. This anointing which covered them both with natural oil and with the Holy Spirit, can be explained simply as God's presence and power at work in, around, and through them. When they cease to be holy and consecrated to God, His Spirit ceases to work in them in the same way.

Likewise, God is asking you to give yourself to Him, as 1 Peter 1:13-16 says, "So prepare your minds for action and exercise self-control. Put all your hope in the gracious salvation that will come to you when Jesus Christ is revealed to the world. So you must live as God's obedient children. Don't slip back into your old ways of living to satisfy your own desires. You didn't know any better then. But now you must be holy in everything you do, just as God who chose you is holy. For the Scriptures say, "You must be holy because I am holy (NLT)."

He Tends our Wounds with Healing Balm

We are empowered more and more to live a holy life as we allow God to come into our brokenness and place His healing balm upon our hearts. Jeremiah 8:21-22 is one of many passages that show He cares about what we're going through. He says, "I hurt with the hurt of my people. I mourn and am overcome with grief. Is there no medicine in Gilead? Is there no physician there? Why is there no healing for the wounds of my people (NLT)?"

Jesus is the perfect representation of God's desire to heal us. Early in our Savior's ministry, He goes into the synagogue in Nazareth and reads from a scroll. In it He was declaring (among other things) that He was anointed with the Holy Spirit to heal the brokenhearted:

The Spirit of the Lord God is upon me, because the Lord has anointed and qualified me to preach the Gospel of good tidings to the meek, the poor, and afflicted; He has sent me to bind up and heal the brokenhearted, to proclaim liberty to the [physical and spiritual] captives and the opening of the prison and of the eyes to those who are bound,

To proclaim the acceptable year of the Lord [the year of His favor] and the day of vengeance of our God, to comfort all who mourn,

To grant [consolation and joy] to those who mourn in Zion—to give them an ornament (a garland or diadem) of beauty instead of ashes, the oil of joy instead of mourning, the garment [expressive] of praise instead of a heavy, burdened, and failing spirit—that they may be called oaks of righteousness [lofty, strong, and magnificent, distinguished for uprightness, justice, and right standing with God], the planting of the Lord, that

> *He may be glorified.*
> *And they shall rebuild the ancient ruins; they shall raise up the former desolations and renew the ruined cities, the devastations of many generations.*
>
> ISAIAH 61:1-4 AMPC
> (SEE ALSO PSALM 147)

The things that steal us from God are often rooted in heartbrokenness. Each of us goes through traumatic events, and the enemy seeks to rush into that place and set up a stronghold. We've talked about removing evil spirits from these places. The anointing is part of what breaks their bondages:

> *It shall come to pass in that day*
> *That his burden will be taken away*
> *from your shoulder,*
> *And his yoke from your neck,*
> *And the yoke will be destroyed*
> *because of the anointing oil.*
>
> ISAIAH 10:27 NKJV

We also need Jesus to bring the oil of joy which overcomes mourning. The Father seeks to give the prodigal parts of our hearts a garment of praise instead of heaviness. We must let Him into the darkness, the sensitive areas, the shameful places that now seek other lovers for comfort. He will shine like the sun, anointing our wounds with His life-giving Spirit. And He will show the deepest parts of us that He is all we ever longed for, so we can overcome what draws us from His consecration.

But for you who fear My name, the sun of righteousness will rise with healing in its wings; and you will go forth and frolic like calves from the stall. And you will crush the wicked underfoot, for they will be ashes under the soles of your feet on the day that I am preparing," says the Lord of armies.

MALACHI 4:2-3 NASB

Pray today:

Heavenly Father, I want to be set apart for You. I'm sorry for how I have gone back to old ways of living and sought to satisfy ungodly desires. I choose to consecrate myself to You again. Please wash me clean, and anoint me with the oil of Your Spirit. Lord Jesus, You know even better than I do where there is wounding in my heart. I invite You to come into these deeply broken places with Your healing balm. Thank You for caring about my pain and desiring to bring redemption. Help me to understand where I have held onto anything ungodly, that has perpetuated walking in unholiness. I choose to release it all to You. Thank You that You will replace mourning and heaviness, with joy and praise. And Your Spirit has come afresh upon me, anointing me with God's presence and power to work in, around, and through me! I pray all this in Jesus's name. Amen!

Journaling Prompt:

Write to God in your own words about how you desire to be

set apart for Him, and ask Him to pour out His healing oil on you. As Jesus seeks to enter your broken heart, He will show you what you need to release. Often you will need to forgive yourself and others. This doesn't mean any person who hurt you is now trustworthy, but that you are not holding onto things that will fester and bring decay. Continuing to forgive and let go allows Jesus to heal in a deeper way, and entrusts Him as Lord over these areas of your heart. Continue to invite Him into these areas whenever you realize you're struggling, or as the Holy Spirit reveals other wounds.

Day 10:

INFILLING OF HIS PRESENCE

> *Create in me a clean heart, God,*
> *And renew a steadfast spirit within me.*
> *Do not cast me away from Your presence,*
> *And do not take Your Holy Spirit from me.*
> *Restore to me the joy of Your salvation,*
> *And sustain me with a willing spirit.*
>
> PSALM 51:10-12 NASB

The Temple and the Glory

WE SEE SEVERAL places in scripture where God fills a place with His glorious presence so strongly that it is undeniable. For example, in Exodus 40:34-38, when the tabernacle was dedicated by Moses, it was covered by a cloud, and God's glory filled it. Then He led His people through the wilderness with the cloud by day and the fire by night.

This wonder of God manifesting His presence, is at times preceded by His people turning away from their sins in repentance, consecrating themselves, and making a sacrificial offering. In response, God's fire and glory comes, and He restores His people to prosperity. This happened in Leviticus 9:22-24 with the tabernacle. And a similar event occurred when the Israelite King Solomon built the Lord a temple made from stone:

> *When Solomon had finished praying, fire came down from heaven and consumed the burnt offering and the sacrifices; and the glory of the Lord filled the temple. And the priests could not enter the house of the Lord, because the glory of the Lord had filled the Lord's house. When all the children of Israel saw how the fire came down, and the glory of the Lord on the temple, they bowed their faces to the ground on the pavement, and worshiped and praised the Lord, saying:*
>
>   *"For He is good,*
>
>   *For His mercy endures forever."*
>
> *... Then the Lord appeared to Solomon by night, and said to him: "I have heard your prayer, and have chosen this place for Myself as a house of sacrifice. When I shut up heaven and there is no rain, or command the locusts to devour the land, or send pestilence among My people, if My people who are called by My name will humble themselves, and pray and seek My face, and turn from their wicked ways, then I will hear from heaven, and will forgive their sin and heal their land."*
>
>   2 CHRONICLES 7:1-3, 12-14 NKJV

John W. Nichols

(See also Exodus 40:34-38, 1 Kings 8, 2 Chronicles 5, Acts 2, Revelation 15:5-8)

As things have drawn us away from the Lord, our fires have dwindled to embers. Scripture shows that God might have even turned His face from us and removed His hand of blessing, to get us to see our need and return to Him. Our repentance, consecration, and offering of our lives as sacrifices (which we have been doing in these previous devotionals), have been preparing us to receive the manifestation of God in our lives again.

His Spirit and His Fire Now Dwells in Us

As we have sought with all our hearts to restore fellowship with God, His glorious presence in the form of His Holy Spirit, and His fire, are ready to come upon us. In Acts 2, as Jesus's disciples prayed and waited for the baptism of the Holy Spirit, His presence filled them, and His fire came over their heads. Then Peter referenced part of Joel 2 in explanation of what was happening.

If we look at this chapter and the one before it, God had sent many trials against His people in order to get them to turn back to Him. When they repented, He blessed them immeasurably:

> *Therefore also now, says the Lord, turn and keep on coming to Me with all your heart, with fasting, with weeping, and with mourning [until every hindrance is removed and the broken fellowship is restored].*
>
> *Rend your hearts and not your garments and*

> *return to the Lord, your God, for He is gracious and merciful, slow to anger, and abounding in loving-kindness; and He revokes His sentence of evil [when His conditions are met].*
>
> *... And I will restore or replace for you the years that the locust has eaten—the hopping locust, the stripping locust, and the crawling locust, My great army which I sent among you.*
>
> *And you shall eat in plenty and be satisfied and praise the name of the Lord, your God, Who has dealt wondrously with you. And My people shall never be put to shame.*
>
> *And you shall know, understand, and realize that I am in the midst of Israel and that I the Lord am your God and there is none else. My people shall never be put to shame.*
>
> *And afterward I will pour out My Spirit upon all flesh; and your sons and your daughters shall prophesy, your old men shall dream dreams, your young men shall see visions.*
>
> *Even upon the menservants and upon the maidservants in those days will I pour out My Spirit.*
>
> JOEL 2:12-13, 25-29 AMPC

Since these verses were fulfilled in Acts 2, the Spirit of the Living God no longer dwells in a temple made by human hands, but in Jesus's followers (1 Corinthians 3:16-17). Please pause, and realize the treasure it is for Him who created all things to live in you! This profound revelation that born-again believers are now God's chosen temple, helped me overcome the things that were pulling my heart away from the Lover of my soul.

We'll talk more tomorrow about the refining fire of God, and today we'll focus on His Spirit. As I began to receive my Creator's love, I also fell more in love with Him. With thankfulness for His Holy Spirit's indwelling, I genuinely didn't want to grieve Him in any way (Ephesians 4:30). How could I continue to carry His Spirit into my sin and ungodly situations, which hurt His heart?

I started winning battles when I drove this fact deeper than head-knowledge, and began to act in faith that the Holy Spirit is my comforter (John 14:26). His comfort truly is greater than the things I eased my pain with. So, I set about making a habit of running to Him instead of drugs, sexual vices, and alcohol.

Despite many failures, I continued trying to seek Him, His love, and His liberty before going to others. Eventually I found it's a million times better to be filled with the Holy Spirit than to be drunk on wine (Ephesians 5:15-21). His presence became more valuable to me than the temporary pleasures of this world.

Desiring Him More Than All Else

Whereas we saw the Holy Spirit come on specific people for times in the Old Testament, because of Jesus's sacrifice and resurrection, we have a better covenant with better promises through faith. The outpouring of the Holy Spirit in Acts chapter 2 continues today. Meaning, just as Jesus's Spirit and fire filled His followers on the day of Pentecost, and several times in Acts—He will fill you.

We must desire God's Spirit more than any other thing. Like the saints of old, we should tell Him, "If Your Presence does not go with me, do not carry us up from here (Exodus 33:15 AMPC)!" And, "A single day in your courts is better than a thousand anywhere else! I would rather be a gatekeeper in the house of my God than live the good life in the homes of the wicked (Psalm 82:10 NLT)."

When we fail, the salvation Jesus afforded those who believe is not weak. We may not easily lose the Holy Spirit's seal on our hearts. But this doesn't mean we can assume we'll experience His manifest presence and anointing no matter how we live. We shouldn't take for granted this gift, trampling on His wonderful grace, seeing all we can get away with. When a Christian partners with other spirits, he's become an unfaithful spouse.

I'm beyond thankful for the times God surprised me by showing up in the midst of my brokenness and depravity. But this shouldn't be the norm. Eventually we need to mature, and get into a position of expecting Him to come. Rather than ignoring God's pleas while running to worldly pleasures, let's prefer a hunger and desire for Heaven. We will be like John the Beloved, who was able to experience all that is written in Revelation, because he kept himself ready.

If we'll live in the Holy Spirit, like John the Revelator, we're readying ourselves to experience Heaven on earth. Before being taken up, he said, "I was in the Spirit [rapt in His power] on the Lord's Day, and I heard behind me a great voice like the calling of a war trumpet, saying, "I am the Alpha and the Omega, the First and the Last (Revelation 1:10-11a AMPC)."

But before we can be rapt in the Holy Spirit's power, we need to be filled (or re-filled). Let's search our hearts again to see if we have turned away from our sins in repentance, consecrated ourselves, and are living as sacrifices unto the Lord. Then we can ask Him to come and fill us and set us on fire for His kingdom and purposes on the earth. Above everything else, we must desire His refining fire, and to live by the sevenfold Spirit of God!

> *The Spirit of the Lord will rest on Him,*
> *The spirit of wisdom and understanding,*
> *The spirit of counsel and strength,*
> *The spirit of knowledge and the fear of the Lord.*
> *And He will delight in the fear of the Lord...*
> ISAIAH 11:2-3A NASB

Pray today:

Jesus, thank You for saving me, and sealing me with Your Holy Spirit. Thank You for dwelling in me and desiring to manifest Your presence with help and blessings in my life. Thank You for comforting me and leading me. Please forgive me for anything I have done that has grieved or quenched Your Spirit, and refine me with Your holy fire.

Spirit of the living God, You are my highest desire. I want You more than anything else I could gain in this world. Would You fill me even more, to overflowing, with Your glorious presence? I want to walk in the ways of the Spirit of the Lord, the spirit of wisdom and understanding, the spirit of counsel and strength, the spirit of knowledge and the fear of the Lord. Thank You, Jesus! It's in Your name, I pray. Amen.

Journaling Prompt:

Write to God and invite Him into every area of your life. Ask for His Spirit and the glory of His presence to fill you. Learn to be comforted by the Holy Spirit and walk in His ways. Dedicate as much time as possible to seek and wait on Him.

You can also dedicate your home to the Lord, and seek for it to be a place where the Holy Spirit wants to manifest. People will come in and sense the presence of God. And when you go out you will carry His Spirit with you, and exhibit His glory to the hungry world.

Remember, I have provided this free PDF that will give some more information and practical advice for being filled with the Holy Spirit and receiving His spiritual gifts. You can get it and the other free gifts mentioned in the Introduction here:

<u>Navigating the Maze of Life with God... As His Child, Filled with His Spirit, and Using His Gifts to Heal the World</u>

<u>GodAndYouAndMe.com/Rekindling-Fire-Free-Stuff</u>

_____
_____
_____
_____

John W. Nichols

Rekindling the Fire

Day 11:

REKINDLING THE FIRE

Now I saw heaven opened, and behold, a white horse. And He who sat on him was called Faithful and True, and in righteousness He judges and makes war. **His eyes were like a flame of fire**, *and on His head were many crowns. He had a name written that no one knew except Himself. He was clothed with a robe dipped in blood, and His name is called The Word of God. And the armies in heaven, clothed in fine linen, white and clean, followed Him on white horses. Now out of His mouth goes a sharp sword, that with it He should strike the nations. And He Himself will rule them with a rod of iron. He Himself treads the winepress of the fierceness and wrath of Almighty God. And He has on His robe and on His thigh a name written:*
KING OF KINGS AND
LORD OF LORDS.

> *... He will baptize you with the Holy Spirit and fire.*
>
> REVELATION 19:11-16 AND MATTHEW 3:11B NKJV (EMPHASIS ADDED)

WE ARE SO blessed to have a glimpse of the awesome revelation of Jesus after His resurrection and ascension in His glorified state. This majestic King with flaming eyes is the one who baptizes us in His Spirit and fire. As Peter proclaimed on the day of Pentecost, "God raised Jesus from the dead, and we are all witnesses of this. Now He is exalted to the place of highest honor in heaven, at God's right hand. And the Father, as He had promised, gave Him the Holy Spirit to pour out upon us (Acts 2:32-33 NLT)..."

> *There appeared to them tongues resembling fire, which were being distributed [among them], and they rested on each one of them [as each person received the Holy Spirit].*
>
> ACTS 2:3 AMP

I have been on fire for the Lord at different points of my life. Looking back they were always amazing times of transformation:

- When I was first born again
- Ten years later when I received an infilling of the Holy Spirit
- When Jesus called me into ministry
- And when I sought after and received a tangible experience of His fire

All of these times set my heart ablaze in different ways. I wish I could say the fire didn't dwindle, but because of my own failures, it has.

How we should desire, seek after, treasure, protect, and stoke His fire, I will never be able to adequately express. This is the beginning of the last half of our devotional. We've done a lot to get to the subject of receiving God's fire, burning with passion for Him again, and keeping it ablaze. Recently we talked about being anointed for holiness and consecration. God is holy, and if you really look into His fire in the Bible, it will give you a healthy fear of Him. But we should not shrink back—because His fire changes everything.

His Fire Cleanses Hands and Purifies Hearts

Who may ascend onto the hill of the Lord?
And who may stand in His holy place?
One who has clean hands and a pure heart,
Who has not lifted up his soul to deceit
And has not sworn deceitfully.
He will receive a blessing from the Lord
And righteousness from the God of his salvation.
This is the generation of those who seek Him,
Who seek Your face...

PSALM 24:3-6 NASB

I believe Jesus was referencing this Psalm in Matthew 5:8 when He said, "Blessed are the pure in heart, for they will see God (NASB)." In our goal of seeking His face and seeing Him, we can't overlook the process of purification. This begins as a free gift by grace through faith in the salvation purchased by Jesus's precious blood. And it continues as we are empowered by grace through faith in His sanctification by His purifying fire.

> *"Behold, I send My messenger,*
> *And he will prepare the way before Me.*
> *And the Lord, whom you seek,*
> *Will suddenly come to His temple,*
> *Even the Messenger of the covenant,*
> *In whom you delight.*
> *Behold, He is coming,"*
> *Says the Lord of hosts.*
> *"But who can endure the day of His coming?*
> *And who can stand when He appears?*
> *For He is like a refiner's fire*
> *And like launderers' soap.*
> *He will sit as a refiner and a purifier of silver;*
> *He will purify the sons of Levi,*
> *And purge them as gold and silver,*
> *That they may offer to the Lord*
> *An offering in righteousness."*
> MALACHI 3:1-3 NKJV

Our hearts are like precious silver mixed with tin and lead, so His fire separates and removes the impurities (Proverbs 17:3 and 25:4). This happens as we continually allow the Father to discipline us in love. If we don't resist Him, He will prune away the branches that are not bearing the fruit of His Spirit in our lives. Though this refining and cutting can be painful, the freedom that we will feel afterwards is more than worth it.

Instead of avoiding His correction, we should run to the Father, showing our trust by submitting to everything He wants to do. And like the disciples in the upper room, we should pray and wait for His Spirit and fire to utterly transform our hearts:

> *"Then I will sprinkle clean water on you, and you will be clean. Your filth will be washed away, and you will no longer worship idols. And I will give you a new heart, and I will put a new spirit in you. I will take out your stony, stubborn heart and give you a tender, responsive heart. And I will put my Spirit in you so that you will follow my decrees and be careful to obey my regulations."*
> EZEKIEL 36:25-27 NLT
> (see also Isaiah 6:1-8, Jeremiah 20:9, Daniel 7:9-10 & 10:5-6, Zechariah 13:9, 2 Corinthians 7:1, Hebrews 9:14, James 1:19-22, 1 Peter 1:5-9, and 1 John 1:5-10)

Fanning Aflame the Fire

One night I woke up on fire. In the dark of my bedroom, I could sense the tangible presence of God, and my whole body felt as if it were burning. For weeks I had been submitting every part of my heart to be rid of all impurities, and seeking Him and His fire. Suddenly He showed up.

This was a definite turning point that occurred about twenty years after beginning my walk with God. I believe it was part of the preparation needed before we could go into the mission field

He was sending us. With it came an extraordinary level of passion and consecration.

I never intended for the fire to wane in my heart, but two years later I was growing cold. Why? Because I had withdrawn again from zealous repentance at the Father's loving rebuke and discipline. I had become like the church in Laodicea:

> *'These things says the Amen, the Faithful and True Witness, the Beginning of the creation of God: "I know your works, that you are neither cold nor hot. I could wish you were cold or hot. So then, because you are lukewarm, and neither cold nor hot, I will vomit you out of My mouth. Because you say, 'I am rich, have become wealthy, and have need of nothing'—and do not know that you are wretched, miserable, poor, blind, and naked—I counsel you to buy from Me gold refined in the fire, that you may be rich; and white garments, that you may be clothed, that the shame of your nakedness may not be revealed; and anoint your eyes with eye salve, that you may see. As many as I love, I rebuke and chasten. Therefore be zealous and repent.*
> REVELATION 3:14-19 NKJV

I didn't realize I was wretched, miserable, poor, blind, and naked. Like the prodigal son who had extravagantly and lavishly expended his father's wealth, I gave it all but was not refilled. How could I be when I took the fruit of the Spirit and disconnected from the vine to "do ministry?" I had to humble myself and come back to the point where I had unknowingly left the Father. I could no longer ignore His discernment about the road I was on and the path He wanted me to return to.

The fire of the Holy Spirit brings power and love and discipline. As I left His disciplines, I became powerless and passionless. And the fear of man brought a spirit of timidity. Upon coming to my senses, I realized I needed to fan into flames again what had become embers.

> *For this reason I remind you to kindle afresh the gift of God which is in you through the laying on of my hands. For God has not given us a spirit of timidity, but of power and love and discipline.*
> 2 TIMOTHY 1:6-7 NASB

Keeping the Fire Burning

Like the lamp in the tabernacle, the holy fire of God in our hearts was never meant to go out:

> *"You shall command the Israelites to provide you with clear oil of beaten olives for the light, to make a lamp burn continually [every night]. In the Tent of Meeting [of God with His people], outside the veil which is in front of the [ark of the] Testimony [and sets it apart], Aaron [the high priest] and his sons shall keep the lamp burning from evening to morning before the Lord. It shall be a perpetual statute [to be observed] throughout their generations on behalf of the Israelites."*
> EXODUS 27:20-21 AMP

Since each of us is now the temple of the Holy Spirit, we must keep our lamps burning for the Lord. Consistently meeting with Him creates an environment for our hearts to be purified, that we would see God and remain on fire. Jesus's anointing of gladness rubs off on us as He heals our wounds. Our lamps overflow with fresh oil of His Spirit. The Father's discipline trims the burnt wick. Then we come away from the secret place, carrying His fragrance of life and shining bright with the light of God.

Pray today:

Jesus, You are awesome, mighty, glorious, and holy! Please search me and purify me with Your refiner's fire. Please cleanse my hands and give me a new heart, that I would be blessed and see You. I long to look into Your eyes of fire! I desire that You would pour out Your Spirit and fire upon me. Help me to not give up praying and waiting until I have received.

Thank You for the times that I have burned with passion and zeal for You. I'm sorry for ever allowing this light within me to wane. I return to my Abba's discipline. I kindle afresh and fan into flames Your holy fire in the lamp of my heart, so that You would raise me up and I would shine forth Your brilliance. In Jesus's name I pray. Amen!

Journaling Prompt:

As the Holy Spirit has convicted and led you into truth through today's devotional, write what you are seeking from Him.

Maybe you have never experienced Jesus's Spirit and fire, or you recognize a need for further sanctification, or you want to see God, or rekindle His holy fire in your heart. He knows and loves you, and desires to give you all these things and more.

Although I have experienced different fillings of the Holy Spirit, His fire, and spiritual gifts, I must admit that my life does not look enough like the book of Acts. I do not let this cause me to doubt or be dismayed. But I continue seeking for more of Him, and I pray you will too.

_____
_____
_____
_____
_____
_____
_____
_____
_____
_____
_____
_____
_____
_____
_____
_____
_____
_____
_____
_____

REKINDLING *the* FIRE

Day 12:

Clothed for Celebration

I will sing and greatly rejoice in Yahweh!
My whole being vibrates
with shouts of joy in my God!
For He has dressed me with salvation
and wrapped me in the robe of His righteousness!
I appear like a bridegroom on his wedding day,
decked out with a beautiful sash,
or like a radiant bride adorned
with sparkling jewels.
In the same way the earth produces its crops
and seeds spring up in a garden,
so will the Lord Yahweh
cause righteousness and praise
to blossom before all the nations!

ISAIAH 61:10-11 TPT

WE HAVE CAST off the old garments, representing previous identities. We have been washed with living water and the precious blood of the Son to remove the filth of our bondages. We have been anointed with the fragrant oil of gladness and the healing balm of Jesus. And we have been given a new spirit and heart with passion for our first love. The time has come for our Heavenly Father to clothe us for a merry festival—His child was dead but now lives!

Dressed with Salvation and Robed with Righteousness

The Bible speaks of many blessings that come upon the righteous. But often I have felt unworthy to receive these benefits because my righteousness is as filthy rags (Isaiah 64:6). Thankfully the Lord knew that there would not be one person who is perfect and able to stand up to His measure of goodness (Ecclesiastes 7:20 and Romans 3:10-18). So He provided His righteousness in place of our lack:

> *Justice is turned back,*
> *And righteousness stands afar off;*
> *For truth is fallen in the street,*
> *And equity cannot enter.*
> *So truth fails,*
> *And he who departs from evil*
> *makes himself a prey.*
> *Then the Lord saw it, and it displeased Him*
> *That there was no justice.*
> *He saw that there was no man,*
> *And wondered that there was no intercessor;*
> *Therefore His own arm*

> *brought salvation for Him;*
> *And His own righteousness, it sustained Him.*
> *For He put on righteousness as a breastplate,*
> *And a helmet of salvation on His head;*
> *He put on the garments of*
> *vengeance for clothing,*
> *And was clad with zeal as a cloak.*
> *According to their deeds,*
> *accordingly He will repay,*
> *Fury to His adversaries,*
> *Recompense to His enemies;*
> *The coastlands He will fully repay.*
> *So shall they fear*
> *The name of the Lord from the west,*
> *And His glory from the rising of the sun;*
> *When the enemy comes in like a flood,*
> *The Spirit of the Lord will lift up*
> *a standard against him.*
> ISAIAH 59:14-19 NKJV

Praise God that He fights for His people! Like this Redeemer of Zion, we are able to put on salvation and righteousness, because of the work of Christ. Not by our own perfection and works, but instead by faith in the only One who was perfect. Therefore, even when we fail, we can rejoice that we have obtained the blessings that come through righteousness because of Jesus.

We are made right with God by placing our faith in Jesus Christ. And this is true for everyone who believes, no matter who we are or what we have done.

> *For everyone has sinned; we all fall short of God's glorious standard. Yet God, in His grace, freely makes us right in His sight. He did this through Christ Jesus when He freed us from the penalty for our sins. For God presented Jesus as the sacrifice for sin. People are made right with God when they believe that Jesus sacrificed His life, shedding His blood.*
>
> ROMANS 3:22-25A NLT

With all our talk of sanctification and holy living, we have to remember that righteousness is a gift from God. Because of His great love for us, and our inability, He made a way for us. Through faith as His child, we are able to put on Christ (Galatians 3:26-27). And despite our weakness, He calls us to clothe ourselves as His representative, and live like Him:

> *Clothe yourselves therefore, as God's own chosen ones (His own picked representatives), [who are] purified and holy and well-beloved [by God Himself, by putting on behavior marked by] tenderhearted pity and mercy, kind feeling, a lowly opinion of yourselves, gentle ways, [and] patience [which is tireless and long-suffering, and has the power to endure whatever comes, with good temper].*
>
> COLOSSIANS 3:12 AMPC

John W. Nichols

Clothe Yourself in Fine Linen, Bright and Clean

Jesus was anointed to proclaim the good news that all can be reconciled to God. We who take Him up on this offer are given garments of praise because our Abba is rejoicing in our return. He has seated us at a special place at the festival table. But this is not with the expectation that we are going to leave the jubilee and go back to our former slave masters. His humbled children will depart, joyfully serving Him in love—and doing righteous acts in His name.

> *And a voice came from the throne, saying, "Give praise to our God, all you His bond-servants, you who fear Him, the small and the great." Then I heard something like the voice of a great multitude and like the sound of many waters and like the sound of mighty peals of thunder, saying, "Hallelujah! For the Lord our God, the Almighty, reigns. Let us rejoice and be glad and give the glory to Him, for the marriage of the Lamb has come and His bride has made herself ready." It was given to her to clothe herself in fine linen, bright and clean; for the fine linen is the righteous acts of the saints. Then he said to me, "Write, 'Blessed are those who are invited to the marriage supper of the Lamb.'" And he said to me, "These are true words of God."*
>
> REVELATION 19:5-9 NASB

As believers consecrate themselves to the Lord out of love, we are preparing the global Church for the coming Bridegroom. Our righteous acts clothe her in bright and clean, fine linen. This doesn't come of our own strength and man-made religious attempts to appease God. How could a duty separate from genuine relationship make a bride ready for marriage?

One of Jesus's main problems with the religious leaders of His day, was their external righteousness, combined with internal deviousness. He saw through their clean clothing, to the darkness of their hearts. He wasn't impressed by their zealous obsession with holding people to impossible and irrelevant standards. They thought they were wise, but couldn't see their God when He came to meet them in the flesh.

Father God desires our heartfelt worship of Him would lead to grace-empowered obedience to His will. This true love and devotion readies us to join in celebration as the Church enters into paradise with her Savior. In joy, Abba is preparing the festivities of our union with Jesus. He is clothing us as a bride in immaculate white. Not just that we would look beautiful for the wedding day, but that we would thoroughly embody the character of Christ—ready to spend eternity with Him!

Pray today:

Praise You, God! You are marvelous, wonderful, and greatly to be praised! Thank You that You have made a way for us to live righteously. We were trapped in dead religion, powerless to overcome sin, and unable to live out our destiny. But You have rescued us! Thank You that when there was none righteous and we could not save ourselves, You armored Yourself with righteousness and salvation, and delivered us from our captors. Thank You, Jesus, that You made a way for us to be saved and that we can put on righteousness by Your sacrifice. And now our only requirement is to lovingly trust You and live from this place of faith.

I want to be like You. I want to be draped with Your attributes as if they were my clothing. I want to put on Christ and Your tenderhearted mercy, kindness, humility, gentleness, and patience. I want to be dressed for the celebration of my Abba, and the wedding feast of the Lamb. I want to be robed in fine linen of righteous acts, born out of wholehearted worship. I want not only to look good externally, but also to be thoroughly perfected in love. As I live my life as a sacrifice to You, I pray it would be my part of preparing the bride for her eternal Husband. I look forward to that day when we will all be gathered together for the greatest celebration. And we will joyfully spend eternity in this blessed union! In Jesus's name I pray. Amen!

Journaling Prompt:

Write to God any ways that You need Him to deepen this revelation and help you to walk it out in love and joy.

_____
_____
_____
_____
_____

Rekindling the Fire

Day 13:

Worshiping in Spirit and Truth

I have refused to walk on any evil path,
so that I may remain obedient to Your word.
I haven't turned away from Your regulations,
for You have taught me well.
How sweet Your words taste to me;
they are sweeter than honey.
Your commandments give me understanding;
no wonder I hate every false way of life.
Your word is a lamp to guide my feet
and a light for my path.
I've promised it once, and I'll promise it again:
I will obey Your righteous regulations.
I have suffered much, O Lord;
restore my life again as You promised.
Lord, accept my offering of praise,
and teach me Your regulations.

PSALM 119:101-108 NLT

JESUS SAID, "GOD is Spirit, and those who worship Him must worship in spirit and truth (John 4:24 NKJV)." We have spoken of His Spirit this week, and also touched briefly on the subject of worship in day 2 of last week. We referenced Romans 12:1 that speaks of dedicating ourselves as living sacrifices, "which is your reasonable (rational, intelligent) service and spiritual ***worship*** (AMPC emphasis added)."

In order to live this life God is calling us to live and worship Him, we need to be people of the spirit and the truth. Besides the infilling of the Holy Spirit, I believe the foundation of this devotion is prayer and the Word of God. These two gifts from the Lord are not only elements of our time in the secret place, but also need to be a normal part of our life. Through them He will reveal Himself and guide us with instruction.

What got the prodigal son into his mess was breaking from a connection with his father. When we want to make our own choices, we can shut off the voice of God, and stop reading His Word. As we come back to Abba, we need to have fellowship with Him and follow His guidance.

> *All Scripture is inspired by God and is useful to teach us what is true and to make us realize what is wrong in our lives. It corrects us when we are wrong and teaches us to do what is right. God uses it to prepare and equip His people to do every good work.*
>
> 2 TIMOTHY 3:16-17 NLT

Getting Back into the Word

When I first gave my life to Jesus, I had tasted and seen the goodness of His written Word, and my passions continued to grow. I couldn't get enough. I was constantly fascinated by the Bible, and allowed it to transform me and increase my faith.

I hate to admit it, but over time my desire diminished. I continued to read the Bible occasionally and without passion, sometimes doing yearly plans, reading mainly with groups of other believers, and in preparation for ministry.

Honestly, theology was a part of my problem. Because as I studied the Word through the lens of man's doctrines and explanations, my fire grew cold. I started to feel like I already knew the Bible. I had God in a reasonable box. When I would read Christian books and come to a verse I knew, I would often skip it. While I am thankful for the foundation I built, I have to say that it was a grave mistake to think my hunger could ever be satisfied.

I have intentionally put the Bible back into my normal schedule, and through this process of repentance and coming back to my Abba, He is giving me deeper revelation again. I also started fasting from social media, choosing to make a habit of going to scripture when I felt the urge to scroll an app on my phone. The wonder I felt as a new believer is returning, and my desire is growing again.

> *However, they did not all heed the good news; for Isaiah says, "Lord, who has believed our report?" So faith comes from hearing, and hearing by the word of Christ.*
>
> ROMANS 10:6-7 NASB

These verses show that you should not only read and hear the Bible, but that you also need to heed God's Word (see James 1:21-

27). As you unite your intake of scripture with faith, you are able to boldly pursue the things of God, and step into the life He's called you to live. This faith will lead to practicing the Word and experiencing a Spirit-led life—girded with truth.

Getting Back into Prayer

Prayer is likely to be an automatic part of the time you devote to meeting with your heavenly Father. This is because it is primarily communicating with Him, by talking to Him and listening to Him. While there may be a way you tend to pray over and over, there are many different kinds of prayer. You might tell God how good He is, ask Him for cleansing and refining, thank Him for what He has done, ask Him to help others, pray for His will to be done in the nations, ask for your needs and godly desires to be met, give Him your worries and request help, and ask Him to lead you.

> *Be anxious for nothing, but in everything by prayer and supplication, with thanksgiving, let your requests be made known to God; and the peace of God, which surpasses all understanding, will guard your hearts and minds through Christ Jesus.*
> PHILIPPIANS 4:6-7 NKJV

This shouldn't only be done in a quiet place, or with your hands clasped and your head bowed, but as a constant dialog with the Holy Spirit all throughout your day. If you talk with Him, He will also try to talk with you. That means you should be listening for His voice every moment.

As you receptively read the Bible, pray without ceasing, hear His still small voice, and obey in the midst of life's circumstances, you will become a living sacrifice. You will begin to worship Him in spirit and truth.

Worship Is an Expression of Love

The deeper you fall in love with God, the more your life will express worship of Him. Loving Him is the key to everything we have been talking about. What tends to steal passion is when two loved ones stop seeking, investing, and engaging in one another. That's why we must seek and find Him through His Word and through prayer—both in and out of the secret place.

Earlier this week I mentioned how God's revelation coming through His spoken and written Word yields growth in your relational knowledge of Him. God is so amazingly good. And as you get to know Him better, you won't be able to help falling in love with Him more. This, combined with your reception of His love towards you, will invoke passion.

The love gushing forth from your innermost being, founded on who He really is, will be like a fountain of worship. You won't be able to keep from praising Him and thanking Him for His goodness and all He has done. In response to your heart, He will manifest His presence with showers of blessings.

Your life commingled with His Spirit will turn into an embodiment of natural worship in spirit and truth. You will join in with King David, shouting, "Lord! I'm bursting with joy over what You've done for me! My lips are full of perpetual praise. I'm boasting of You and all Your works, so let all who are discouraged take heart. Join me, everyone! Let's praise the Lord together.

Let's make Him famous! Let's make His name glorious to all (Psalm 34:1-3 TPT)."

Pray today:

Abba, thank You for the treasure that is Your written and spoken Word. I desire to receive it. I'm sorry for the ways that I have neglected reading the Bible and not sought You thoroughly enough in prayer. Please reignite a passion within me to pursue revelation through Your holy scriptures, and through deep fellowship with You.

I desire to fall more and more in love with You. And this passion will cause me to talk with You constantly and hide Your Word in my heart. I know that this will bring growth in faith and lead me to step into Your destiny for my life.

I lay my everything down again, desiring to worship You in spirit, in truth, and as a living sacrifice. Help this worship to be a genuine expression of my whole being, pouring out passion. Let me receive Your love and Your Spirit, and respond with heartfelt praise and thanksgiving. In Your Son's holy name I pray, amen!

Journaling Prompt:

Write to God about any help needed in the areas of prayer, regularly reading the Bible, and genuine worship. Is there anything you could fast from for a season to make room for incorporating these habits in your life? Journal with Him about these things, how you want them to spring out of love, and try to plan some action steps.

REKINDLING *the* FIRE

Day 14:

RESTORED AS A BELOVED CHILD

"Wake up, wake up, O Zion! Clothe yourself with strength. Put on your beautiful clothes, O holy city of Jerusalem, for unclean and godless people will enter your gates no longer. Rise from the dust, O Jerusalem. Sit in a place of honor. Remove the chains of slavery from your neck, O captive daughter of Zion. ... How beautiful on the mountains are the feet of the messenger who brings good news, the good news of peace and salvation, the news that the God of Israel reigns! The watchmen shout and sing with joy, for before their very eyes they see the Lord returning to Jerusalem. Let the ruins of Jerusalem break into joyful song, for the Lord has comforted his

> *people. He has redeemed Jerusalem. The Lord has demonstrated his holy power before the eyes of all the nations. All the ends of the earth will see the victory of our God."*
> ISAIAH 52:1-2, 7-10 NLT

THIS AMAZING PROPHECY reveals God's good plans for Jerusalem. On the surface, it may seem it has nothing to do with us, but it is actually extremely relevant and foretells of our destiny. A couple of days ago in the Clothed for Celebration devotional, we referenced the preparation of the bride of the Lamb. In Revelation 21 this bride of Christ is shown to be a New Jerusalem and that is what the prophet Isaiah was declaring.

These verses show how God will display His might while rescuing Zion and returning her to His original design. In Jeremiah 2:2-3, God says to Jerusalem, "I remember regarding you the devotion of your youth, Your love when you were a bride, Your following after Me in the wilderness, Through a land not sown. Israel was holy to the Lord, The first of His harvest. All who ate of it became guilty; Evil came upon them (NASB)."

If you continue reading in Jeremiah, it shows that Jerusalem (and the rest of Israel) became unfaithful to God, with the adulterous worship of other gods, and committed all kinds of horrible sin. We might not like the thought, but this is how we became when we lost our first love (Revelation 2:4) and put other things above God in our hearts.

The prophetic words of Isaiah, though, are not only God's good plans for Jerusalem, but also a picture of how He desires to restore each one of us. Just as He will remake Jerusalem, He is redeeming us upon our return to Him and placing us in a seat of honor. This recreated heavenly city is where we as believers will live when we overcome the world and enter into glory.

> *"Now I saw a new heaven and a new earth, for the first heaven and the first earth had passed away. Also there was no more sea. Then I, John, saw the holy city, New Jerusalem, coming down out of heaven from God, prepared as a bride adorned for her husband. And I heard a loud voice from heaven saying, "Behold, the tabernacle of God is with men, and He will dwell with them, and they shall be His people. God Himself will be with them and be their God. And God will wipe away every tear from their eyes; there shall be no more death, nor sorrow, nor crying. There shall be no more pain, for the former things have passed away."*
> *... "Come, I will show you the bride, the Lamb's wife." And he carried me away in the Spirit to a great and high mountain, and showed me the great city, the holy Jerusalem, descending out of heaven from God, having the glory of God. Her light was like a most precious stone, like a jasper stone, clear as crystal."*
>
> REVELATION 21:1-4, 9B-11 NKJV
>
> (the whole chapter is very powerful and encouraging, verses 5-9a only left out for brevity)

REKINDLING *the* FIRE

Donning Sandals that Carry the Good News

I find it interesting that our opening verse from Isaiah mentions putting on beautiful clothes, as we talked about previously. It also says that the feet of those who carry the good news of peace with God and His salvation—are beautiful. Remember how the Father gives His returning prodigals sandals (Luke 15:22)? When we are restored to Abba as His children, we are given shoes to stand firm in our redemption and carry the gospel message to others.

> *... having strapped on your feet the gospel of peace in preparation [to face the enemy with firm-footed stability and the readiness produced by the good news].*
> EPHESIANS 6:15 AMP
> (part of the full armor of God
> from verses 10-18)

> *"Everyone who calls on the name of the Lord will be saved."*
> *How then are they to call on Him in whom they have not believed? How are they to believe in Him whom they have not heard? And how are they to hear without a preacher? But how are they to preach unless they are sent? Just as it is written: "How beautiful are the feet of those who bring good news of good things!"*
> ROMANS 10:13-15 NASB (SEE ALSO 2 CORINTHIANS 5:17-21)

As the Father sent His Son Jesus into the world to preach repentance and the coming kingdom of God—He is sending us. He has washed our feet, declared them beautiful, and given us shoes to stand against the enemy's lies. As His empowered representatives, we are mandated to carry the gospel to the ends of the earth.

Putting on the Ring of a King

Jacob, who God renamed Israel, in the Old Testament had many sons whose descendants later became the twelve tribes of Israel. Some of these sons became jealous of their brother Joseph, sold him to slave-traders, and convinced their father that he had died. Although Joseph went through many trials, including slavery in Egypt, false accusation, and being forgotten in prison, he remained faithful to the Lord.

Joseph ended up having an opportunity to interpret some dreams of the Pharaoh, and God used this to raise him to a position of governing the land. He gave him wisdom and favor which saved Egypt and the surrounding areas during a long famine. In this redemption story God took what was meant for evil and used it to protect and provide for Joseph's family, who He had destined to be His very own people.

> *Pharaoh said to Joseph, "See, I have set you over all the land of Egypt." Then Pharaoh took his signet ring off his hand and put it on Joseph's hand; and he clothed him in garments of fine linen and put a gold chain around his neck. And he had him ride in the second chariot which he had; and*

> *they cried out before him, "Bow the knee!" So he set him over all the land of Egypt.*
> GENESIS 41:41-43 NKJV

Like a prince of Egypt, Joseph was given Pharoah's signet ring that showed he had the highest position in the government. These types of rings in ancient times meant the wearer represented a family or kingdom. They would have a special insignia that would leave an impression when the ring was pressed into a seal of wax or clay. This would act as a signature of the ring's wearer and showed their authority.

Joseph, who had been a slave and prisoner, was quickly raised up to essentially the highest rank in the land. Likewise, when the prodigal son received the ring of his father, it showed he was restored to a position of authority in his home (Luke 15:22). We too were enslaved but have left our captors and returned to our loving Abba. Though we don't deserve it, He has given us authority in His kingdom as joint-heirs with Christ.

> *Now we're no longer living like slaves under the law, but we enjoy being God's very own sons and daughters! And because we're His, we can access everything our Father has—for we are heirs because of what God has done!*
> GALATIANS 4:7 TPT (SEE ALSO ROMANS 8:12-19)

We began these devotionals by looking at Romans 8 and recognizing we have been given the Spirit of adoption and are able to call God, Abba, as His children. We also saw that although this position was given as a free gift by faith, and not through our own righteous works, there was an expected condition of us living in and by the Holy Spirit. So we have left the ways of this world and the flesh, and are learning the ways of the Spirit.

Since that first devotional we have been taking steps to walk this out, by returning to the Father's loving discipline, removing what held us in bondage, receiving the Holy Spirit and His fire, and being prepared to reveal God's glory as His children (Romans 8:18-19). This has not just been about escaping hell and obtaining heaven when we die, but about coming into our destiny.

Like Jesus, we want to actually live out the identity of a child of God in relationship with the Father. He is the first of many brethren, and His Spirit is conforming us to His image. By faith, it is no longer we who live, but Christ is living through us. We are being raised up to sit with Him and manifest His glory in the earth!

Pray today:

Thank You, Abba, that You have recreated me like the New Jerusalem. I have left the other lovers of my heart and returned to my first love. Thank You for washing my feet and sending me as Your messenger to proclaim the good news of Your redemption (John 13:12-16). Thank You for strapping my feet so that I can stand and resist evil (Ephesians 6:13-15). Thank You for placing a ring on my finger, showing that I belong to You and am a joint-heir with Your only begotten Son.

Jesus, I can't fully express how thankful I am that You

have shared Your inheritance with me. I know this wasn't just so I can be with You when I die. You want me to be like You in this life. I want to walk with Our Abba, and talk with Him, and represent Him as His child. Please help me to do this, reflecting Your glory for all the world to see. Thank You, Lord! I pray all of this in Your glorious name, Jesus. Amen!

Journaling Prompt:

Address God with thanksgiving for all He has provided you. Ask Him to help you believe and receive these blessings and continue living out these truths with steps of faith!

_____
_____
_____
_____
_____
_____
_____
_____
_____
_____
_____
_____
_____
_____
_____
_____
_____

John W. Nichols

Congratulations on completing the second week of this twenty-one-day devotional!

We have come a long way to rekindle the fire. Going through these devotionals for my own growth and passion, I have taken time to really receive each subject before moving on. I want to be sure I'm able to impart this truth, not only from a theological perspective, but also from the heart. When the Father says, "Let's prepare a great feast and celebrate... And everyone celebrated with overflowing joy (Luke 15:23a-24b TPT)," I want to actually enter into His joy as I wave you to also come to the table!

In the 3rd week we will jump into the joy and blessings of being restored and on fire for God. We'll also look at what the Father says in Luke 15:23-24. Get ready to fan yourself into even greater flames with the following topics:

- We were Dead in Sin, but Now We Are Living as the Son
- Receiving the Blessings of Being a Child of God
- Manifesting the Holy Spirit
- Burning Bright with More Passion and Zeal
- Becoming Sensitive to the Things of the Spirit
- Changing the World through Friendship with God
- Looking Forward and Stepping into Our Destiny

Day 15:

LIVING AS THE SON

And you were dead in your offenses and sins, in which you previously walked according to the course of this world, according to the prince of the power of the air, of the spirit that is now working in the sons of disobedience. Among them we too all previously lived in the lusts of our flesh, indulging the desires of the flesh and of the mind, and were by nature children of wrath, just as the rest. But God, being rich in mercy, because of His great love with which He loved us, even when we were dead in our wrongdoings, made us alive together with Christ (by grace you have been saved), and raised us up with Him, and seated us with Him in the heavenly places in Christ Jesus, so that in the ages to come He might show the boundless riches of His grace in kindness toward us in Christ Jesus. For by grace you have been saved through faith; and this is not of yourselves, it is the gift of God; not a result of works, so that no one may boast. For we are His

> *workmanship, created in Christ Jesus for good works, which God prepared beforehand so that we would walk in them.*
>
> EPHESIANS 2:1-10 NASB

From Death to Life Abundant

AS PRODIGALS RETURN home, most probably haven't realized they were walking as dead men. Not only was the prodigal son considered dead to the family (because of his betrayal), spiritually he had died as well. But upon his arrival, his father joyfully proclaimed, "My son was dead and is alive again; he was lost and is found (Luke 15:24a NKJV)."

Our opening verses show that we were all dead in sin at one time. The world is not aware of this fact. Our coworkers, neighbors, family, and friends may think they are living the good life, all the while headed to destruction. But God's grace has invited us all to receive true life in Christ, and by faith we have taken it. That is why the Father has given His children shoes that are prepared with the gospel of peace. So that we can share what He has done for us, to this lost and decaying world.

We were captives of a death-sentence, but Jesus has ransomed us by taking the punishment our sin prescribed. He purchased us with His precious blood, placed His Spirit in us, and our lives are now His:

> *Have you forgotten that your body is now the sacred temple of the Spirit of Holiness, who lives in you? You don't belong to yourself any longer, for the gift of God, the Holy Spirit, lives inside*

your sanctuary. You were God's expensive purchase, paid for with tears of blood, so by all means, then, use your body to bring glory to God!
1 CORINTHIANS 6:19-20 TPT

Jesus offers us abundant life (John 10:10) and shows us how to glorify God. Our old lives apart from Him, even in our own good deeds and self-righteousness, only equated to death. That is why when we joined with Christ in faith, our sinful lives went into the grave with Him. And through His resurrection we have received a new life, empowered to overcome:

For when we died with Christ we were set free from the power of sin. And since we died with Christ, we know we will also live with Him. We are sure of this because Christ was raised from the dead, and He will never die again. Death no longer has any power over Him. When He died, He died once to break the power of sin. But now that He lives, He lives for the glory of God. So you also should consider yourselves to be dead to the power of sin and alive to God through Christ Jesus.
ROMANS 6:7-11 NLT
(See also verses 1-6, and Galatians 2:20)

Transforming to His Glorious Image

The same Spirit who raised Christ from the dead lives in us (Romans 8:11). He has raised us to life with Jesus and given us liberty—freedom over the power of sin. We have been recreated in Him for good works. In fact, our new lives are expected to be continually transformed to look like His.

> *Now the Lord is the Spirit, and where the Spirit of the Lord is, there is liberty [emancipation from bondage, true freedom]. And we all, with unveiled face, continually seeing as in a mirror the glory of the Lord, are progressively being transformed into His image from [one degree of] glory to [even more] glory, which comes from the Lord, [who is] the Spirit.*
> 2 CORINTHIANS 3:17-18 AMP

Our opening scripture passage shows that we have been seated with Christ. The Father has placed us in a seat of honor at the celebration of our return. We are going to talk more about this later and what it has to do with our destiny. For now, I want to highlight that He doesn't want us to sit where we don't belong.

Abba has adopted us, given us His signet ring, and called us joint-heirs with His perfect Son. But not with the thought that we would remain dead. If we will submit to the Spirit He has given us, we will actually be transformed to look like Jesus. We may start out as newborn babies, and no less God's children, but we are meant to mature into full-grown adults.

The New Testament which was written in Greek, uses different words which refer to different stages of sonship. *Teknion* (Strong's 5040) for instance, means a dearly loved little child. Whereas, *huios* (Strong's 5207) typically connotes a mature son (male or female) who shares in the likeness of their heavenly Father. There are even more nuances which can provide revelation. If we study them, we'll find that we are expected to grow in maturity, character, and ability to sit in this honorable place—where Christ is seated.

> *If then you were raised with Christ, seek those things which are above, where Christ is, sitting at the right hand of God. Set your mind on things above, not on things on the earth. For you died, and your life is hidden with Christ in God. When Christ who is our life appears, then you also will appear with Him in glory.*
> COLOSSIANS 3:1-4 NKJV

We may feel unworthy to carry His glory, because when we look at the earth and our old lives, we see death. But we have to remember that our old lives are gone. The transcription of our sin was nailed with Jesus on the cross. With His resurrection power, He has washed us completely clean. So rather than focus on our unworthiness, we need to look up at Him, and even see ourselves in Him.

Our lives now should be lived from the position of being seated with Christ. Jesus was honored and raised up in power, authority, and glory, as He glorified the Father with His earthly life (John 17:1-5). Now as we glorify Him, He raises us up in honor and glory too (John 17:22-24). This is not at all that we would be worshiped. We carry His glory so that people will know we came from Him as we display His goodness.

We have to begin thinking from this heavenly perspective. As we look to His kingdom, we see abundant life. As we fix our gaze on Jesus's glorious face, His fiery eyes guide us, and we begin to reflect Him. We are transformed to carry His glory, so the Father can be known and His will can be done through us on the earth!

Pray today:

Jesus, thank You for humbling Yourself and putting aside Your glory to live as a servant. You lived the perfect life that we could not, and then died the death that we deserved. Thank You for taking my sin on the cross. Thank You for carrying my old life into the grave, and that I was resurrected with You into new life, by the power of the Holy Spirit. My sinful ways were crucified with You, and I am learning Your ways, seated by Your side in Heaven.

Thank You, Holy Spirit, that You help me to walk in the good works prepared for me. You have given me liberty and are transforming me to look like Jesus. Please help me to keep my eyes on things above and live from the position of being seated with Christ. I desire to reflect Him, carry His glory, live the life You created me to live, and lead others to the Father. I will take steps of faith to live this abundant life. Thank You, Lord. In Jesus's name I pray, amen!

Journaling prompt:

Write to God and ask Him to help you not only believe these truths from scripture, but also to walk them out. As you are going about your life, try to live as one who reflects Jesus.

_____
_____

John W. Nichols

Day 16:

Joyful Satisfaction in Him

*In Jerusalem, the Lord of Heaven's Armies
will spread a wonderful feast
for all the people of the world.
It will be a delicious banquet
with clear, well-aged wine and choice meat.
There He will remove the cloud of gloom,
the shadow of death that hangs over the earth.
He will swallow up death forever!
The Sovereign Lord will wipe away all tears.
He will remove forever all insults and mockery
against His land and people.
The Lord has spoken!
In that day the people will proclaim,
"This is our God!
We trusted in Him, and He saved us!*

> *This is the Lord, in whom we trusted.*
> *Let us rejoice in the salvation He brings!"*
>
> ISAIAH 25:6-9 NLT

THE HONORED SEAT at Abba's banqueting table shows He has restored our favor and identity before others. He instructed His servants to kill the fatted calf, meaning that we are receiving His abundant blessings. He is cheering the return of His beloved child with out-poured gifts, and so His provision is restored along with our sonship. After all, we have declared to Him that He is our portion and it's His presence that brings us true happiness.

> *"O Lord, You are the portion of my inheritance and my cup; You maintain my lot. The lines have fallen to me in pleasant places; Yes, I have a good inheritance. I will bless the Lord who has given me counsel; My heart also instructs me in the night seasons. I have set the Lord always before me; Because He is at my right hand I shall not be moved. Therefore my heart is glad, and my glory rejoices; My flesh also will rest in hope. For You will not leave my soul in Sheol, Nor will You allow Your Holy One to see corruption. You will show me the path of life; In Your presence is fullness of joy; At Your right hand are pleasures forevermore."*
>
> PSALMS 16:5-11 NKJV

Though the Lord is holy, and can be serious and jealously angry, He also laughs, celebrates, and is absolutely joyful. His goodness is displayed in so many ways. Like His unfailing love, the creation of human pleasure, and blessings that come in the midst of living as a sacrifice. We experience the fullness of joy when we encounter Him at the seeking of His face. In His presence, He bids us to stay and be satisfied by the provision in His hand.

A Table Set with Goodness and Joy

Like our opening scripture passage, there are so many verses in the Bible that mention the Lord setting up a feast for His people (Psalm 23:5-6, Revelation 3:20, and Luke 14:15-23 are a few examples). The fact of the matter is we make our heavenly Father smile, and He enjoys being with us. As we worship and live our lives in reverential awe of Him, He wants us to delight in His goodness:

> *O taste and see that the Lord [our God] is good! Blessed (happy, fortunate, to be envied) is the man who trusts and takes refuge in Him.*
> *O fear the Lord, you His saints [revere and worship Him]! For there is no want to those who truly revere and worship Him with godly fear.*
> *The young lions lack food and suffer hunger, but they who seek (inquire of and require) the Lord [by right of their need and on the authority of His Word], none of them shall lack any beneficial thing.*
> PSALM 34:8-10 AMPC

There was a point in history where God's people, the

Israelites, had turned away from Him and were taken into captivity for many years. The book of Nehemiah describes when some of them were allowed to return to Jerusalem and rebuild the wall in the midst of surrounding threats. After finishing this work, God was honored and worshiped publicly. The scriptures were opened and taught to the people probably for the first time in that generation. In humility they fell down to their knees, and worshiped God with their faces to the ground.

> *"... all the people were weeping when they heard the words of the Law. Then he said to them, "Go, eat the festival foods, drink the sweet drinks, and send portions to him who has nothing prepared; for this day is holy to our Lord. Do not be grieved, for the joy of the Lord is your refuge."*
> NEHEMIAH 8:9B-10 NASB

It was not their fasting, or the ramparts, which provided them security. The joy of the Lord was their strength. Throughout the Old Testament, the people who followed God prospered and enjoyed His benefits of favor and overcoming their enemies. This inheritance is ours as well. We only have to rely on Him, find bliss in His presence, and relish in His goodness.

Taste and See

God has many blessings which will satisfy mankind's desperate hunger. Jesus taught His disciples to ask Abba for daily bread, which has more than one meaning. While they needed the Father's supply for their physical nourishment, this bread also represented their reliance on His Word, and His healing deliverance (Matthew 4:4 and Matthew 15:21-28).

Jesus's first miracle was turning water into wine. Later He confused the religious leaders by hanging out with worldly people and apparently eating and drinking whatever He wanted (Luke 7:33-35). The Bible warns us not to be drunk or participate in the sinful parties of the world (Ephesians 5:18 and 1 Peter 4:3). But as He befriended sinners, Jesus remained pure (1 Peter 2:22 and 2 Corinthians 5:21), even while eating and drinking with them.

> *You send rain on the mountains*
> *from your heavenly home,*
> *and you fill the earth with the fruit of your labor.*
> *You cause grass to grow for the livestock*
> *and plants for people to use.*
> *You allow them to produce food from the earth—*
> *wine to make them glad,*
> *olive oil to soothe their skin*
> *and bread to give them strength.*
> PSALM 104:13-15 NLT
> (see also Joel 2:21-24 and Ecclesiastes 9:7-8)

Like the bread analogy above, many benefits from God are likened to food. Such as the teaching of His Word being described as milk to the newborn believer, and solid food to the mature son (Hebrews 5:11-14, 1 Corinthians 3:1-3, 1 Peter 2:1-3. The King James Version says meat instead of solid food.) Things like this and the fruit of the tree of life, new wine of joy, oil of gladness, living water, honey, salt, the bread of life, and others are mentioned throughout the Bible—often with deep meaning.

> *But **the fruit** produced by the Holy Spirit within you is divine love in all its varied expressions:*
> > *joy that overflows,*
> > *peace that subdues,*
> > *patience that endures,*
> > *kindness in action,*
> > *a life full of virtue,*
> > *faith that prevails,*
> > *gentleness of heart, and*
> > *strength of spirit.*
>
> *Never set the law above these qualities, for they are meant to be limitless.*
>
> GALATIANS 5:22-23 TPT
> (EMPHASIS ADDED)

As we host the Holy Spirit's presence we are transformed from within. If we will cultivate this ***fruit,*** our character will emanate love, joy, peace, patience, kindness, goodness, faithfulness, gentleness, and self-control. We are not the only ones called to taste and see this sweetness of God's Spirit. The fruit of His work in our lives is meant to be enjoyed by others, so they too can behold His love.

The Lord's Table

> *Then Jesus said to them, "Most assuredly, I say to you, unless you eat the flesh of the Son of Man and drink His blood, you have no life in you. Whoever eats My flesh and drinks My blood has eternal life, and I will raise him up at the last day. For My flesh*

is food indeed, and My blood is drink indeed. He who eats My flesh and drinks My blood abides in Me, and I in him. As the living Father sent Me, and I live because of the Father, so he who feeds on Me will live because of Me. This is the bread which came down from heaven—not as your fathers ate the manna, and are dead. He who eats this bread will live forever."

JOHN 6:53-58 NKJV

These words of Jesus turned many people away, but He was not condoning cannibalism. Those who had ears to hear knew He was referring to something representative and spiritual. He was also prophesying of His last meal with His disciples, when He instituted an act of remembrance we call Communion, or the Lord's table (Matthew 26, Mark 14, Luke 22, 1 Corinthians 11:17-34, Acts 2:42-47). Jesus's body was crucified taking our death, and He shed His blood for the cleansing of our sins. His eternal life was offered to all who would wholeheartedly place themselves in His hands.

*Like an apple tree among the trees of the forest,
So is my beloved among the young men.
In his shade I took great delight and sat down,
And his fruit was sweet to my taste.
He has brought me to his banquet hall,
And his banner over me is love.*

SONG OF SOLOMON 2:3-4
NASB

Ultimately God calls you to eat and drink of Him. Nothing compares to Him. Nothing satisfies your longing like Him. In His love, He calls you to sit with Him and spreads His blessings to be feasted upon. Come to His table. Taste and see that He is good. And invite the world to join with you in joyful celebration.

Pray today:

Jesus, thank You for desiring to commune with me and coming to the door of my heart and knocking. I open up myself and invite You to come in and for us to feast together (Revelation 3:20). I want to eat and drink Your bread of life and living water. I want to take in the life You lived in the flesh and drink the wine of the joy of my salvation.

Abba, thank You for setting a table before me, even in the presence of my enemies (Psalm 23:5-6). That You invite me to sit under celebratory banners of love. That Your bountiful provision would be displayed as my cup runs over. That I would taste the fruit of Your Spirit and be changed forever.

I will sit and eat from Your living Word—milk, honey, and meat. And my life will be like seasoning salt, causing people to thirst after You (Matthew 5:13). Thank You that I am not the only one invited to this banqueting table. You have called me to, "Go out quickly into the streets and lanes of the city, and bring in here the poor and the maimed and the lame and the blind."

And I will say, "Master, it is done as you commanded, and still there is room." Then the master will say to me His servant, "Go out into the highways and hedges, and compel them to come in, that my house may be filled (Luke 14:7-23 NKJV)." You are amazing, wonderful, glorious, majestic, holy, and worthy! I will invite the world to come, taste, and see that You are absolutely good! In Jesus's name I pray. Amen!

Journaling prompt:

Write to God, in your own words, how you want to taste these good things from Him, bear the fruit of His Spirit, and joyfully invite others to join you at His table.

My family often takes Communion together in our home and as a regular part of ministry. This does not only have to be done by an ordained minister, in a church, and with special unleavened bread. You can use any kind of bread or cracker, and juice or wine. Pray over these elements and bless them as representing Jesus's body and blood.

It can be helpful to read 1 Corinthians 11:17-34, and other scriptures about what was provided to us through Jesus's blood, crucifixion, and resurrection. Ask the Holy Spirit to search you and reveal anything that you need to submit to Him or repent of. Proclaim the blessings of Jesus's perfect life lived in His body for you, the stripes He took on His back for your healing, and His blood which washes you absolutely clean. Proclaim His resurrection power which overcame sin and the sting of death in your life.

REKINDLING *the* FIRE

Communion is extremely deep, and if you continue to meditate on it and related subjects throughout scripture, you will realize and apprehend even more benefits that Jesus has provided through it. You can also pray and ask God to reveal and give you the benefits of other symbolic foods in scripture. Sometimes I feel led to hold out my hands and receive what He wants to give me. I have had some amazing encounters and profound experiences with God as I bring His spiritual drinks and foods to my physical mouth to partake as a prophetic act.

John W. Nichols

Day 17:

MANIFESTING THE HOLY SPIRIT

But the manifestation of the Spirit is given to each one for the profit of all: for to one is given the word of wisdom through the Spirit, to another the word of knowledge through the same Spirit, to another faith by the same Spirit, to another gifts of healings by the same Spirit, to another the working of miracles, to another prophecy, to another discerning of spirits, to another different kinds of tongues, to another the interpretation of tongues. But one and the same Spirit works all these things, distributing to each one individually as He wills.

1 CORINTHIANS 12:7-11 NKJV

AS JESUS WAS finishing His race on earth, before He ascended to heaven, He passed the baton to His disciples. In His final instructions and prayers, we read that Jesus spoke also of those who would come to faith through their race which advanced His kingdom. Many sections of scripture show that He was clearly speaking of generations—which eventually lead to your and my story. We have been passed the baton from those ahead of us, and now we have a circuit to run.

This continuation of Abba's work through all His adopted children is shown in Acts. Upon receiving the baptism in the Spirit and fire, Peter told the crowd, "... you will receive the gift of the Holy Spirit. For the promise is for you and your children and for all who are far off, as many as the Lord our God will call to Himself (Acts 2:38b-39 NASB)." And we see Philip is a prime example of the Holy Spirit's powerful ministry expanding to those who were not Jesus's original Apostles (Acts 8:4-8).

We have been talking about representing the Son by the transformation of the Holy Spirit. This internal work has the potential to overflow into a supernatural manifestation of His love to touch the people around us. It's His grace upon them as well as within us through power from On High to continue the work Jesus gave His disciples (Luke 24:49 and Acts 1:8). Our opening verses show that the gifts of the Holy Spirit are given to each one and for the benefit of all!

However, as we have become like prodigals, have we continued to receive and practice these benefits? Just like God does not force us to be saved, it's very rare that things of the spirit happen automatically and without our involvement. God desires that we engage and join with Him by faith, in the same way that Jesus attributed people's faith to their reception of healing. The gifts of the Spirit also require our faith-filled involvement.

John W. Nichols

Partnering with the Holy Spirit

Immediately on the heels of 1 Corinthians 13's famous chapter on love, the Apostle Paul writes:

> *"Pursue [this] love [with eagerness, make it your goal], yet **earnestly desire and cultivate the spiritual gifts** [to be used by believers for the benefit of the church], but especially that you may prophesy [to foretell the future, to speak a new message from God to the people]. For one who speaks in an unknown tongue does not speak to people but to God; for no one understands him or catches his meaning, but by the Spirit he speaks mysteries [secret truths, hidden things].*
> 1 CORINTHIANS 14:1-2 AMP
> (EMPHASIS ADDED)

In the verses above we are told to earnestly desire and cultivate spiritual gifts. Many Christians are waiting on God to take over their body before they will believe that spiritual gifts are for them. We would not be told to earnestly desire something that only depends on God's will. And we wouldn't be told to cultivate something that we couldn't invest in and see an increase.

In this chapter, Paul shows that he is able to choose when to pray in the spirit or with his understanding. He gives the gift of prophecy a higher recommendation. He also gives instructions to the church on when to do what. This all means that the Holy Spirit is not taking absolute control of us but rather desires our partnership. We are able to seek to be graced with spiritual gifts. We have the ability to stop and start the gifts of the Spirit with which we are graced. And we can invest faith, time, and discipline to see an increase in these blessings of the Holy Spirit.

Some things that didn't help the waning of my passions was a decrease in spiritual disciplines. I was not regularly spending time with the Father, reading the Word, fasting, and praying with my understanding and in tongues. All of these activities require, prove, and increase our faith. We've talked about restoring each of them except praying in a heavenly language, which we will discuss below.

I believe we should seek God for each spiritual gift. It's not so we can have supernatural experiences and cool stories to tell. But these blessings are for the Spirit of God to manifest in our lives only as He can. His gifts are a breaking into our natural realm, enabling us to minister in His power.

Praying in the Spirit

When the day of Pentecost came as Jesus's disciples were waiting for the promise of God's power, suddenly the Holy Spirit came in as a mighty wind, tongues of fire appeared over their heads, and they began to speak in other languages. People from many different regions heard these believers declaring the truth about God in their own native tongues. As these disciples went out from there spreading the gospel, they continued to see others baptized in the Holy Spirit and speak in new tongues as well.

So far we've restored the foundation and the more natural disciplines. This helps us to be in a better place of faith to receive and practice the gifts of the Spirit. However, we haven't waited to discuss the gift of tongues, praying in the spirit, and heavenly languages because they are of less importance. In fact, these things build yourself up and allow you to pray and proclaim the perfect will of God.

> *A person who speaks in tongues is strengthened personally, but one who speaks a word of prophecy strengthens the entire church.*
> *I wish you could all speak in tongues, but even more I wish you could all prophesy. For prophecy is greater than speaking in tongues, unless someone interprets what you are saying so that the whole church will be strengthened.*
> 1 CORINTHIANS 14:4-5 NLT
> (SEE ALSO JUDE 1:20-21)

This and other verses in this chapter show that speaking in tongues is not normally understood except by the gift of interpretation of tongues. Although we can't usually understand it, and prophecy is a more beneficial gift in the gathering of believers, each person who is able to speak in tongues strengthens themselves spiritually. This is extremely valuable for the transformation of every believer, because it helps us come into God's plan for our lives.

> *Now in the same way the Spirit also helps our weakness; for we do not know what to pray for as we should, but the Spirit Himself intercedes for us with groanings too deep for words; and He who searches the hearts knows what the mind of the Spirit is, because He intercedes for the saints*

> *according to the will of God.*
> ROMANS 8:26-27 NASB

I never quit this practice, but I fell out of the discipline of purposefully setting aside time to just pray in the Spirit. When I committed a daily hour of fervently using my prayer language again, I could see an immediate benefit. At times my wife and I would pray a certain amount of time every hour on the hour, or a set time every evening with the whole family. It doesn't have to be a specific way, but I encourage you to pray in the Spirit as much as possible.

There is really too much to say about these gifts of tongues, but I wanted to at least dip into the subject. When digging into the Bible, you can find it shows there are different types of tongues. I hope you will seek God to understand and receive what you can. If you have not prayed in a heavenly language before, I will have some more practical information after the prayer and journaling prompt.

Gifts of the Spirit

We shouldn't limit the wonderful ministry of the Holy Spirit to lists we have gleaned. But the Bible helps us by showing examples and letting us know some of what's available. When we read of Jesus and His disciples, as well as people in the Old Testament, operating in many of these gifts—we should expect to do the same by the Holy Spirit within.

I will give a brief explanation of the list found in 1 Corinthians 12:8-10, but it will not do it justice. You should seek God for His revelation and understanding.

- The word of wisdom — speaking something that gives God's enlightenment and direction beyond your own ability
- The word of knowledge — God making you aware of something you didn't know, often revealing His knowledge and care for a person or situation
- The gift of faith — having supernatural faith without a hint of doubt, which causes believing in, acting upon, and receiving the things of God
- Gifts of healings — receiving and facilitating the benefit of God's healing and deliverance in many ways and in various situations
- Working of miracles — the natural is able to be quickly overridden by the supernatural in an awe-inspiring way
- The gift of prophecy — receiving hidden revelation from God, sometimes about something that has not happened yet, and proclaiming this and His unfolded mysteries
- Discerning of spirits — recognizing good or evil that is at work, sometimes accompanied by seeing or knowing what's happening in the spiritual realm
- Different kinds of tongues — speaking, singing, or praying a language which you did not learn naturally, whether a tongue of another nation, tongues of angels, or prayer language in perfect agreement with God
- The interpretation of tongues — understanding words that were spoken in tongues, whether your

own or another person's, and speaking out what was said
- Other gifts are mentioned in Romans 12:6-8 and Ephesians 4:7-13

These are your inheritance as a restored manifest child of God. All are meant for Abba's will to be accomplished, should be done in love, bring His freedom and healing, and encourage and edify people, places, and situations. Ask your Heavenly Father for each of these spiritual gifts to manifest in your life as the need arises. As you step out in faith and regularly practice operating in these gifts, you will see an increase in the Holy Spirit's power at work in and through you.

Pray today:

Father God, please bless me with empowerment from On High. Jesus, I pray that I would be filled afresh with Your Spirit, Your fire, and a heavenly language would bubble up from within! Holy Spirit, I pray that Your power would manifest in my life to bless those around me!

Please increase my faith, that You desire to work in me all these things so that I can be used to bless the world around me. I earnestly desire every one of Your spiritual gifts, especially that I would prophecy. Please help me to cultivate these gifts. That I would invest time, faith, and discipline to practice them and see an increase! In Jesus's name I pray. Amen!

Journaling prompt:

Write to God about how you want His Spirit to work in and through you, and to help you seek after and invest in His spiritual gifts. Ask Him for the gifts you want to see more of in your life.

Some people have the gift of tongues easily spring up from them like a fountain. Some need to overcome things that are inhibiting the flow of the Spirit. If this is your scenario, go to God about it and honestly allow Him to deal with any issues. Because of previous theological teaching, it was very hard for me to initially receive and operate in the things of the Spirit. I had to purposefully renounce bad teaching and the fear of being strange, and speak in faith and agreement with God's Word.

I asked for prayer from a trusted pastor when I knew God was trying to get me to receive but I was struggling. Then I had to choose to open my mouth and begin to speak in faith the little foreign words that I seemed to have in my head. At first it was a tiny babbling brook of baby talk, but eventually with faith, time, and practice it became a flood of heavenly language that transformed my life!

Often the things of the spirit are more subtle than what we imagine when we are reading scripture. Pay attention to the promptings, nudges, feelings that you have where the Holy Spirit may be leading you to step out in faith. I've seen God bless me and my family with these spiritual gifts in many ways at many different times. They definitely benefit us personally. But I have to say they flow more abundantly when I'm ministering to other people. If you feel like you want to see an increase, begin to practice them with others. The Lord really will use you to touch people in powerful ways!

John W. Nichols

Day 18:

BURNING BRIGHT

*I was in the Spirit [rapt in His power] on the
Lord's Day, and I heard behind me a great voice
like the calling of a war trumpet,
Saying, I am the Alpha and the Omega, the First
and the Last.* **Write promptly what you see (your
vision) in a book and send it to the seven
churches** *which are in Asia—to Ephesus and to
Smyrna and to Pergamum and to Thyatira and to
Sardis and to Philadelphia and to Laodicea.
Then I turned to see [whose was] the voice that
was speaking to me, and on turning
I saw seven golden lampstands,
And in the midst of the lampstands [One] like a
Son of Man, clothed with a robe which
reached to His feet and with a
girdle of gold about His breast.
His head and His hair were white like white wool,
[as white] as snow, and*
**His eyes [flashed] like a flame of fire.
His feet glowed like burnished (bright) bronze as**

> *it is refined in a furnace,* and His voice
> was like the sound of many waters.
> In His right hand He held seven stars, and from
> His mouth there came forth a sharp two-edged
> sword, and His face was like the sun
> shining in full power at midday.
> When I saw Him, I fell at His feet as if dead. But
> He laid His right hand on me and said, Do not be
> afraid! I am the First and the Last,
> And the Ever-living One [I am living in the
> eternity of the eternities]. I died, but see, I am
> alive forevermore; and I possess the keys of death
> and Hades (the realm of the dead).
> Write therefore the things you see, what they are
> [and signify] and what is to take place hereafter.
> As to the hidden meaning (the mystery) of the
> seven stars which you saw on My right hand and
> the seven lampstands of gold: the seven stars are
> the seven angels (messengers) of the seven
> assemblies (churches) and **the seven lampstands
> are the seven churches.**
>
> REVELATION 1:10-20 AMPC
> (EMPHASIS ADDED)

JESUS IS THE head of the Church, and we are members of His body (Ephesians 1:22-23, Romans 12:4, and 1 Corinthians 12:13). This omnipotent and omnipresent God of Love wants to bless the world, and we are the ones He uses to do it. Let's get into a position to really be His hands and feet.

Refined to Perfection

Our opening verses show that we, the Church, are the lampstands. Jesus warns these seven churches that He will remove their lampstands if they do not heed His instructions. We shouldn't think we are above the need to hear and obey. We must ensure we stay lit. It's in our obedience that we are perfected, like the book of Hebrews speaks of Jesus:

> *In the days of His humanity, He offered up both prayers and pleas with loud crying and tears to the One able to save Him from death, and He was heard because of His devout behavior. Although He was a Son, He learned obedience from the things which He suffered. And having been perfected, He became the source of eternal salvation for all those who obey Him, being designated by God as High Priest according to the order of Melchizedek.*
> HEBREWS 5:7-10 NASB
> (see also Hebrews 7:28 and Luke 13:31-32 in NKJV)

Jesus's feet were perfect, and yet they were refined (Revelation 1:15). He was proved by His submission to the Holy Spirit and completion of the task His Father had given Him. As He submitted His will to the Father before going to the cross, we must copy His devout behavior and prayers to the One who can save us. We too as children are being refined through what we suffer by following our Abba's directions.

We live by faith as the feet of Jesus, and we're also perfected. We are being refined as bronze purified by fire. He makes us a part of His priesthood (Revelation 5:9-10). As His lamps, we burn bright carrying God's radiance into dark places. With joy our faces reflect the beams of Abba's glory, saying, "Come! Be reconciled to God. The Son has made a way for you to come. Return to your everlasting Father!"

Stoking the Fire

Are there any believers in your fellowship suffering great hardship and distress? Encourage them to pray! Are there happy, cheerful ones among you? Encourage them to sing out their praises! Are there any sick among you? Then ask the elders of the church to come and pray over the sick and anoint them with oil in the name of our Lord. And the prayer of faith will heal the sick and the Lord will raise them up, and if they have committed sins they will be forgiven.

Confess and acknowledge how you have offended one another and then pray for one another to be instantly healed, for tremendous power is released through the passionate, heartfelt prayer of a godly believer!

Elijah was a man with human frailties, just like all of us, but he prayed and received supernatural answers. He actually shut the heavens over the land so there would be no rain for three and a half years! Then he prayed again and the skies opened up over the land so that the rain came again and produced the harvest.

Finally, as members of God's beloved family, we must go after the one who wanders from the truth and bring him back. For the one who restores the sinning believer back to God from the error of his way, gives back to his soul life from the dead, and covers over countless sins by their demonstration of love!

JAMES 5:13-20 TPT

As we follow our great High Priest, Jesus, He leads us to look and behave like Him. He calls us to act as priests in ministering God's will to the hurting world. Whether that looks like encouragement, joyful praise, supernatural healing, fallen nature submitting to God's plans, or one sinner coming back to the Father, we with human weaknesses are representing the perfect, all-powerful, and loving Abba.

One area where I have struggled is keeping passion, zeal, and fervency. This is a major problem, as we read, "tremendous power is released through the passionate, heartfelt prayer of a godly believer (verse 16 TPT)!" The King James Version puts it this way, "The effectual fervent prayer of a righteous man availeth much."

Every Biblical character, including the prophet Elijah, was a normal person. Yet God used their earnest prayers in marvelous ways. How might He use us as we stoke the fire for more heartfelt passion, and zealously fight for His will to be done?

I have personally seen the difference in the effectiveness of weak prayers, and what comes out of fanning myself into flames. When we stir up the Spirit and make authoritative declarations the demons tremble, sickness flees, and what was out of alignment comes into order. Some of us need to get out of our comfort zone. Get loud. Get passionate. And proclaim the will of God like we mean it!

Set on Fire and Watched Burn

If we cooperate with Him, Jesus will set His Church on fire. Starting with the day of Pentecost, there have been revivals throughout Church history where God moved through His people in powerful ways. We know about many of these historical moves of God, but surely not all. They have started by sparks of the Holy Spirit catching thirsty hearts and growing into blazing wildfires.

Some common elements of revival are:

- A recognition that God has manifested in a special and prolonged way, and people are drawn from all around to come into His presence
- Often ignited by a person or group devoting themselves to seeking God wholeheartedly in prayer and consecration
- There is freedom of the move of the Holy Spirit, Who brings conviction of sin, and many recognize their need for repentance
- People's passions for God are kindled afresh, and that moment marks a turning point in their lives with long-lasting positive change
- The Lord's transformative touch is not only experienced locally but expands to other churches and communities

Often the Lord will use one person, two, or a small group of people to start these uncontrollable fires. Many of these revivalists have been willing to be different, kicked out of denominations, and minister wherever the wind of the Spirit carried them. They get alone with God, groaning with a deep hunger, and wait on Him until He moves in the area and in their hearts. When they feel the stirring of the Holy Spirit and His flaming fire within, they take it to those who seek after the living God.

> *His word was in my heart like a burning fire shut up in my bones; I was weary of holding it back, and I could not.*
> JEREMIAH 20:9B NKJV

The question is, are we willing to be used in this way. Are we willing to wait on Jesus and follow Him into uncomfortable places? Are we willing to stand when everyone else is sitting, and zealously proclaim what the Spirit of the Lord is saying? Are we willing to let Him set us on fire and draw others to watch us burn?

Pray today:

> *Jesus, You are the head and Your Church is Your body. I pray that You would have Your way in Your Church, starting with me. I want to be Your hands and feet. Please refine me like burnished bronze, that I would walk in obedience to the Father. I want to be like a golden lampstand, useful as Your instrument, shining light into dark places.*

I want to be a part of Your Church who represents You to the world. Even in my weakness, help me to encourage others, change the atmosphere to one of praise, allow Your healing to flow, overcome the natural, and lead others to know You. Please help me to stoke Your fire within for more passion and zeal. Please help me to pray fervently and proclaim the truth with heartfelt boldness. Please set me on fire, so that I can burn bright for You, and be the spark of Your revival! I pray all this in Your holy name. Amen!

Journaling prompt:

You know the areas where you have struggled with the concepts outlined in today's devotional. Take some time to journal these to God. Ask Him to help you know what practical steps you need to take to fan yourself into flames and walk this out!

_____
_____
_____
_____
_____
_____
_____
_____
_____
_____
_____
_____
_____

John W. Nichols

Day 19:

BECOMING SENSITIVE TO THE SPIRIT

*I pray that the Father of glory, the God of our
Lord Jesus Christ, would impart to you the riches
of the Spirit of wisdom and the Spirit of
revelation to know Him through
your deepening intimacy with Him.
I pray that the light of God will illuminate the
eyes of your imagination, flooding you with light,
until you experience the full revelation of the
hope of His calling—that is, the wealth of God's
glorious inheritances that He finds in us,
His holy ones!
I pray that you will continually experience the
immeasurable greatness of God's power made
available to you through faith. Then your lives
will be an advertisement of this immense power as*

> *it works through you! This is the mighty power
> that was released when God raised Christ from
> the dead and exalted Him to the place of highest
> honor and supreme authority
> in the heavenly realm!*
>
> EPHESIANS 1:17-20 TPT

THE APOSTLE PAUL wrote in the beginning of Romans that when a person gives into the trappings of this world and submits to spirits of deception, God eventually releases their minds into corruption (Romans 1:18-32). For the next two chapters he goes on to show that all are guilty, the law could not save us, but that we are justified by faith in Christ (Romans 3:21-26).

Just as the prodigal son was dead and is now alive because of his return to the father, our spiritual senses were deadened, but now are being revived. We were under a depraved mind, but now can proclaim with the man Jesus healed, "One thing I know: that though I was blind, now I see (John 9:25b NKJV)."

Instead of living in a state of doubt, fear, and confusion, everything is becoming clear. We are learning how to hear Yeshua's voice again, and join ours with His in speaking verily in love. We are learning how to be sensitive to His Spirit, and take faith-filled, obedient steps into all truth. We are learning how to be in tune with heaven, so Abba's will can be done on earth.

Eyes to See and Ears to Hear

Our opening verses show that God desires to flood the eyes of our hearts with enlightenment, wisdom, and revelation. This comes through intimate knowledge of Him and leads to hope in His calling. He is unfolding the mystery of our inheritance and His great power at work in and through us. This is humanly impossible to understand, but Jesus is opening our eyes and ears.

> *Ears to hear and eyes to see—*
> *both are gifts from the Lord.*
> PROVERBS 20:12 NLT

Speaking to His disciples, which now includes you and me, our Redeemer answered why He spoke in parables, "To you it has been granted to know the mysteries of the kingdom of heaven, but to them it has not been granted... Therefore I speak to them in parables; because while seeing they do not see, and while hearing they do not hear, nor do they understand... But blessed are your eyes, because they see; and your ears, because they hear (Matthew 13:11, 13, & 16 NASB, see also John 10:27)."

As we have been turning away from the things that have blinded us, Jesus is giving us revelation. When I was given over to alcohol, I couldn't see how the "spirits" were manipulating me (pun intended). But now that I have freedom, any returning temptation is quite clear. Even more wonderful is the ability to recognize the work of God.

> *Blessed are the pure in heart,*
> *For they shall see God.*
> MATTHEW 5:8 NKJV

These eyes to see and ears to hear are not just an ability to understand the Bible or to recognize the spiritual roots of natural manifestations. You can also actually see God. This is scriptural as we read such testimonies by the prophets. Do you believe you're able to have similar experiences (James 5:16-18)? Take in the words of John the Beloved, and imagine yourself seeing and hearing what he described:

> *After this **I looked, and behold**, a door standing open in heaven! And the first voice which **I had heard, like the sound** of a [war] trumpet speaking with me, said, "Come up here, and **I will show** you what must take place after these things." At once I was in [special communication with] the Spirit; and **behold**, a throne stood in heaven, with One seated on the throne. And He who sat there **appeared like** [the crystalline sparkle of] a jasper stone and [the fiery redness of] a sardius stone, and encircling the throne there was a rainbow that **looked like** [the color of an] emerald.*
> REVELATION 4:1-3 AMP
> (EMPHASIS ADDED)

Spiritual Senses

All of our natural senses are shadows of what God gave us first in the spirit and what mankind had at creation. I believe that Adam and Eve were aware of more than what we can perceive now, but this sensitivity was lost with the fall. While our spirits can still recognize the angelic and demonic, something normally blocks that information from connecting to our bodies and souls.

Thankfully Jesus, who is the last Adam, came to restore us back to what God originally intended. He has given us His Spirit and instructs us to walk in Him, rather than in the flesh (Romans 8:5-17). When we join with Him in the sharpening of our sensitivity to the Spirit we can be led by Him, and go deeper and deeper in His revelation:

> *Concerning this we have much to say which is hard to explain, since you have become dull in your [spiritual] hearing and sluggish [even slothful in achieving spiritual insight]. For even though by this time you ought to be teaching others, you actually need someone to teach you over again the very first principles of God's Word. You have come to need milk, not solid food. For everyone who continues to feed on milk is obviously inexperienced and unskilled in the doctrine of righteousness (of conformity to the divine will in purpose, thought, and action), for he is a mere infant [not able to talk yet]! But solid food is for full-grown men, for those whose senses and mental faculties are trained by practice to discriminate and distinguish between what is morally good and noble and what is evil and contrary either to divine or human law.*
>
> HEBREWS 5:11-14 AMPC

We are supposed to be sharp in hearing and quick in spiritual insight. A key is becoming experienced and skilled in understanding righteousness, and the ongoing discipline of following the Holy Spirit's lead. This helps us to discern good and evil and opens the door to training our senses. We can actually practice recognizing what is happening in the spiritual realm.

A Sanctified Imagination

Jesus has begun this work, and we are being transformed from glory to glory to think, see, and hear as He did. But like we discussed in Day 6, our thoughts often need to be captured and brought into obedience (2 Corinthians 10:3-5). The things of this world that we have taken in like the news, movies, books, music, magazines, podcasts, games, you-name-it have filled our minds with all sorts of ungodly pictures and ideas.

The gates of our eyes and ears need to be cleansed with the blood of Christ, living water, and His anointing oil. Our imaginations need to be purified. We need Jesus's fire to burn away the images of our old life that still haunt us. The things we never should have seen or heard, or taken part in. The false prophecies not placed by the Holy Spirit in our hearts.

God intended our imagination to be like His. He molded us in His image and breathed life into us. And unlike everything else He had made, He gave us the ability to create. To see something in our minds, to believe in its possibility, and to bring it forth. I am not only speaking of the natural ability to plan, invent, build, and physically make something. Spiritually, we empower the things we believe in, and by faith we draw them in—whether good or evil.

> *What I always feared has happened to me. What I dreaded has come true.*
> JOB 3:25 NLT

John W. Nichols

For as he thinks within himself, so is he.
PROVERBS 23:7A TPT

Jesus answered saying to them, "Have faith in God. Truly I say to you, whoever says to this mountain, 'Be taken up and cast into the sea,' and does not doubt in his heart, but believes that what he says is going to happen, it will be granted him. Therefore I say to you, all things for which you pray and ask, believe that you have received them, and they will be granted you."
MARK 11:22-24 NASB
(see also Hebrews 11, Proverbs 18:21, and Deuteronomy 30:19-20)

Our minds need to be transformed and renewed with the Word (Romans 12:2, John 17:17, and Ephesians 5:26). While we are waiting on the Lord, if our imagination is lead astray, we miss the opportunity to receive from the Spirit. It's often initially in our thoughts that we perceive what is sensed spiritually. As we see ourselves taking part in the pages of scripture, we can enter into actual experiences. When we picture receiving something from our Abba, we have faith, and then it happens.

When putting the things in today's devotional to practice, I have had the supernatural overwhelm my natural senses. I have smelled heaven come into the room. I have tasted scrolls given by angels. I have heard Jesus's voice like the sound of many waters. I have felt the Father's cloud of glory, and seen His good plans for my future.

Pray today:

Father of glory, please impart to me the riches of the Spirit of wisdom and the Spirit of revelation. Please illuminate the eyes of my imagination, and flood me with light. I want to experience deep intimacy with You, Your full revelation, the hope of Your calling, my glorious inheritance in You, and the mighty power You are releasing in and through me!

Holy Spirit, please help me to be sharp in hearing, quick in spiritual insight, and grow in maturity to be able to receive more from You. I repent of being inexperienced and unskilled in understanding righteousness, and the times that I have not followed Your lead. I am turning around and desire to discern good and evil, to train my senses, and practice recognizing what is happening in the spiritual realm. Please help me most of all to be sensitive to You and Your guidance.

Jesus, I want to have Your mind and put on the way You think. Please cleanse me of all the ungodly things I have tasted, seen, smelled, felt, and heard by Your precious blood, living water, and Your anointing oil. Please purify and refine my thoughts, feelings, imagination, and creativity with Your holy fire. I want to perceive and receive everything You want to show me in Your Word, in what's really happening around me, and in the heavenly realms. Thank You, Lord, it's in Your name that I pray. Amen!

Journaling prompt:

Write to God and thank Him for the times He has revealed things to you, whether it was by natural means or supernatural. We must not forget what He has done and what we have experienced through His Spirit. Sometimes people or the enemy belittle these things with unbelief and doubt, but if we recognize them instead of discrediting them it opens ourselves to receive more. Also write to God any things You need to repent of, what needs to be purified, and anything that you would like to experience by the Holy Spirit.

When you are able to be secluded and uninterrupted, take time to sit comfortably, close your eyes, quiet your thoughts, and wait on the Lord. You might hear a word, feel a sensation, smell or taste something pleasant, or see something in your thoughts. Anything you perceive, look for more of what surrounds it, and feel free to ask the Holy Spirit about it. God is absolutely good, and what you experience from Him will be life-giving. Even if He is bringing correction, He will also give you hope, peace, and encouragement.

If you sense or imagine things that oppose Jesus's nature and the Bible, it could be from your own soul or the enemy. Just deal with it as we have talked about previously. Speak out loud commanding anything ungodly to go in the name of Jesus, speak to your body that it can relax but is not tired and doesn't need to fall asleep, speak to your soul to focus on the Lord and bless Him, speak to your spirit that you want to be completely in tune with the Holy Spirit. Don't give up, continue waiting with joy and expectation, and praise Abba even before you experience anything. Be thankful and act in faith for the smallest of encounters with Him, and you will grow in being able to receive more and more.

Some of the free resources I've linked before will help in this area. I have an audio teaching on ways God speaks to us, how to practically listen to Him, and act on what He says. Also, there is a PDF on some keys to having a quality devotional time with God. Get them here:

GodAndYouAndMe.com/Rekindling-Fire-Free-Stuff

_____
_____
_____
_____
_____
_____
_____
_____
_____
_____
_____
_____
_____
_____

John W. Nichols

Day 20:

CHANGING THE WORLD

No one has greater love [no one has shown stronger affection] than to lay down (give up) his own life for his friends. You are My friends if you keep on doing the things which I command you to do. I do not call you servants (slaves) any longer, for the servant does not know what his master is doing (working out). But I have called you My friends, because I have made known to you everything that I have heard from My Father. [I have revealed to you everything that I have learned from Him.]

JOHN 15:13-15 AMPC

YESTERDAY WE TALKED about Jesus opening our eyes and ears and becoming sensitive to His Spirit. While He was in His earthly ministry, Jesus only did what He "saw" His Father doing (John 5:19). And He tells His disciples that He has made known to them everything He "heard" from the Father. Jesus is offering us to be a part of His inner circle. Although we have returned to the Father, truly humbled as bondservants, He says essentially, "I am calling you a friend instead of a servant because you are invited into the dialog between Abba, Myself, and Holy Spirit."

It's in this intimate heavenly council that we hear instructions, His commandments, and show our love through faith-filled obedience. Jesus summed up all the commandments with love (Mark 12:28-34), and His great love was expressed as He gave His life on the cross in obedience to the Father. Likewise, we show our love to God and others through responding in faith, laying down our lives, and doing what we hear and see Abba doing.

Equipping to Overcome

Our opening verses took place in the midst of the words Jesus spoke before going to the cross, recorded in the end of John chapter thirteen through chapter seventeen. He gave His disciples many instructions which will also equip us to overcome and change the world according to the Father's will:

- ***Love*** — Jesus gave His disciples a new commandment to love one another. He also said if we love Him, we will keep His commandments and follow His word, and His Father will love us and make Their dwelling in us. He said to remain in His love, and the greatest love is shown by laying down your life. Because we love and believe in Jesus, He said the Father loves us. And He asked in prayer for the love between Him and the Father from the foundation of the world to be in us. (John 13:25-35, 14:15, 14:23-24, 15:8-17, 16:26-27, 17:22-26)

- ***The World*** — Our Messiah said that all people would know His disciples because of their love. He said the evil ruler of the world was coming but had nothing in Him. And the world would know Jesus loved the Father because He did exactly as He was commanded. He said because His disciples are not of the world, but chosen by Him, the world will hate and persecute us. Despite this, the Holy Spirit will help us testify about Jesus. And His Spirit will also convict the world of sin, righteousness, and judgment. He gave all these instructions so we would have peace, even in the midst of trials, Jesus has overcome the world. Finally, He says while we are in the world, not to be of it, and we will be protected from the evil one, so that the world would know about His love and that we were sent by Him. (John 13:35, 14:30-31, 15:18-27, 16:8-11, 16:33, 17:13-26)
- ***Good Works*** — The Savior told His disciples He was returning to His Father, and to believe by His works that He had come from the Father. He told them whoever believes in Him would do even greater works than He did. He said if we do not remain in Him, we can do nothing, but if we abide in Him we will bear much fruit. And while Jesus was praying He said He had glorified the Father

by accomplishing the work He had given Him to do. (John 14:10-12, 15:1-11, 17:4)
- ***Asking the Father*** — Jesus said a few times that we could ask the Father anything in His name and He would do it. He also said this can come out of our direct connection with the Father because He loves us. (John 14:13-14, 15:7, 16:23-28. This idea is also shared in other gospels and 1 John 5:13-15.)
- ***The Holy Spirit*** — Christ reassured His disciples that He was not leaving them alone but sending His Spirit. He described Him as a Helper who will remain in us forever, teach us all things, and remind us of what He has said. He called Him the Spirit of truth who comes from the Father, and said He would testify about the Son. Though they didn't want Jesus to go, He said it's advantageous for us that He return to the Father, otherwise the Helper would not come. He said though His disciples couldn't bear everything He wanted to teach them, the Holy Spirit would guide them into all truth. And the Holy Spirit doesn't speak on His own accord, but will show what is to come, glorifies the Son, and discloses to us what belongs to Him. (John 14:16-17, 14:26, 15:26-27, 16:5-15)

Our faith in Christ, our expression of love through obedience, and our connection with the Father, Son, and Holy Spirit gives us the ability to speak as a friend to Jesus and make requests. These also help us as we navigate this world, having victory over its snares, and blessing it with God's love at work in us.

John W. Nichols

Transforming the World with the Gospel

We see the disciples following these last instructions from Jesus in the book of Acts. They asked the Father as they had need and were filled with the Holy Spirit on many occasions. Though they faced persecution in beatings, stonings, imprisonments, and death, they continued doing good works and showing the world the love and power of Christ. Paul, who was added to the apostles, also carried the gospel into the major regions of the world in this way. After completing His missionary journeys into areas where Christ was not known, he wrote to believers in Rome:

> *Now may the God of hope fill you with all joy and peace in believing, so that you will abound in hope by the power of the Holy Spirit.*
> *And concerning you, my brothers and sisters, I myself also am convinced that you yourselves are full of goodness, filled with all knowledge and able also to admonish one another. But I have written very boldly to you on some points so as to remind you again, because of the grace that was given to me from God, to be a minister of Christ Jesus to the Gentiles, ministering as a priest the gospel of God, so that my offering of the Gentiles may become acceptable, sanctified by the Holy Spirit. Therefore in Christ Jesus I have found reason for boasting in things pertaining to God. For I will not presume to speak of anything except what Christ has accomplished through me, resulting in the*

> *obedience of the Gentiles by word and deed, in the power of signs and wonders, in the power of the Spirit; so that from Jerusalem and all around as far as Illyricum I have fully preached the gospel of Christ. And in this way I aspired to preach the gospel, not where Christ was already known by name, so that I would not build on another person's foundation; but just as it is written:*
>
> *"They who have not been told about Him will see, And they who have not heard will understand."*
>
> *For this reason I have often been prevented from coming to you; but now, with no further place for me in these regions, and since I have had for many years a longing to come to you whenever I go to Spain—for I hope to see you in passing, and to be helped on my way there by you, when I have first enjoyed your company for a while—but now, I am going to Jerusalem, serving the saints.*
>
> ROMANS 15:13-25 NASB

Here Paul is testifying about what Jesus had done in and through him which we have the joy of reading in the book of Acts and the letters he wrote to the churches. At the time of writing this, Paul didn't know that he would be jailed for the gospel in Jerusalem, sent to Rome as a prisoner, and there martyred for his faith. He and the other disciples of Christ were transforming the known world. In the face of every opposition, they truly gave up their lives, took up their crosses, and followed their Savior who had gone ahead of them—even to the point of death.

John W. Nichols

Turning the World Upside Down

As Jesus had warned, the world would not accept His followers, but this didn't stop them from obeying the Holy Spirit. Before the passage we read from Romans, before any of Paul's writings, he had a dream which instigated his second missionary journey.

> *That night Paul had a vision: A man from Macedonia in northern Greece was standing there, pleading with him, "Come over to Macedonia and help us!" So we decided to leave for Macedonia at once, having concluded that God was calling us to preach the Good News there.*
> ACTS 16:9-10 NLT

He and Silas first spent some time in Philippi, where God provided favor and lodging with a woman named Lydia. This became the beginnings of a new church. But when Paul cast out a spirit of divination from a young slave girl, the owners angrily brought him and Silas to the town leaders, and they were severely beaten and thrown in prison. Despite this, Paul and Silas praised God, and suddenly an earthquake opened all the jail doors and unshackled everyone. The jailer assumed the prisoners had escaped and fearfully decided to kill himself, but Paul stopped him and shared with him the love of Christ, and he and his household were all saved.

The next town they went to was called Thessalonica, where Paul immediately went to preach the gospel in the Jewish synagogue. Some Jews, a multitude of devout Greeks, and many leading women came to faith in Christ. But some were not happy, and assembled a mob which attacked the place where Paul had been, saying, "These who have turned the world upside down have come here too... these are all acting contrary to the decrees of Caesar, saying there is another king—Jesus (Acts 17:6b and 7b NKJV)." The reputation of the early Church was on the rise, and the ruler of this world was not happy.

Paul and Silas had to quickly leave the city, but when we read 1 Thessalonians, we see that the church thrived despite many trials. If we will also faithfully follow the lead of the Holy Spirit, God can take small lives and small connections, and change the world. There is another King named Jesus, and though every other king will do anything to stay enthroned, we must not give in or give up. He has overcome, and it's time for this generation to turn the world upside down as well. We also have to be willing to show His great love by laying down our lives, taking up our crosses, and following Him in changing the world.

Pray today:

Thank You, Jesus, that You no longer call me a servant, but a friend. I will continue to do the things which You command. Thank You for all You've given us to overcome and change the world. I'm sorry for the fear I have had of those who can destroy my body, instead of the honor I can give to the One who holds my soul. I'm sorry for any time that I have wasted when my life was meant to be spent on You. I'm sorry for any way I have held back because of doubt that You could use me too.

You showed the greatest love. You laid down Your life so

John W. Nichols

Your enemies could be saved—even to make me Your friend. I am receiving Your instructions and Your Spirit, and I will show my love by obeying Your commands. You said, love God and love my neighbor. I want to do that well. Help me to follow You, wherever You lead, speak what You say, and show all people Your love. Help me to change the world, no matter the cost. I pray this all in Your holy name, Jesus. Amen!

Journaling prompt:

Sit with the Holy Spirit for some time and allow Him to minister this message to you. Write anything He reveals and anything He is prompting you to do.

Today's devotional was extremely difficult to write, but upon the breakthrough my heart was touched deeply by the Holy Spirit. I felt a strong conviction for when I have chosen not to lay down my life. I pray that you will feel this burden from the Lord, but that it would be a joy. After all, Jesus shows that the Father's discipline, and our faith-filled obedience—lead to joy:

As for us, we have all of these great witnesses who encircle us like clouds. So we must let go of every wound that has pierced us and the sin we so easily fall into. Then we will be able to run life's marathon race with passion and determination, for the path has been already marked out before us. We look away from the natural realm and we focus our attention and expectation onto Jesus, who birthed faith within us and who leads us forward into faith's perfection. His example is this: Because His heart was focused on the joy of knowing that you would be His, He endured the agony of the cross and conquered its humiliation, and now sits exalted at the right hand of the throne of God!

So consider carefully how Jesus faced such intense opposition from sinners who opposed their own souls, so that you won't become worn down and cave in under life's pressures. After all, you have not yet reached the point of sweating blood in your opposition to sin. And have you forgotten His encouraging words spoken to you as His children? He said,

> *"My child, don't underestimate the value*
> *of the discipline and training of the Lord God,*
> *or get depressed when He has to correct you.*
>
> *For the Lord's training of your life*
> *is the evidence of His faithful love.*
> *And when He draws you to Himself,*
> *it proves you are His delightful child."*

Fully embrace God's correction as part of your training, for He is doing what any loving father does for his children. For who has ever heard of a child who never had to be corrected? We all should welcome God's discipline as the validation of authentic sonship. For if we have never once endured His correction it only proves we are strangers and not sons.

And isn't it true that we respect our earthly fathers even though they corrected and disciplined us? Then we should demonstrate an even greater respect for God, our spiritual Father, as we submit to His life-giving discipline. Our parents corrected us for the short time of our childhood as it seemed good to them. But God corrects us throughout our lives for our own good, giving us an invitation to share His holiness. Now all discipline seems to be painful at the time, yet later it will produce a transformation of character, bringing a harvest of righteousness and peace to those who yield to it.

So be made strong even in your weakness by lifting up your tired hands in prayer and worship. And strengthen your weak knees, for as you keep walking forward on God's paths all your stumbling ways will be divinely healed!

HEBREWS 12:1-13 TPT

Rekindling the Fire

Day 21:

LOOKING FORWARD

And I saw between the throne (with the four living creatures) and the elders a Lamb standing, as if slaughtered, having seven horns and seven eyes, which are the seven spirits of God sent out into all the earth. And He came and took the scroll out of the right hand of Him who sat on the throne. When He had taken the scroll, the four living creatures and the twenty-four elders fell down before the Lamb, each one holding a harp and golden bowls full of incense, which are the prayers of the saints.
And they sang a new song, saying, "Worthy are You to take the scroll and to break its seals; for You were slaughtered, and You purchased people for God with Your blood from every tribe, language, people, and nation. You have made them into a kingdom and priests to our God, and they will reign upon the earth."
Then I looked, and I heard the voices of many angels around the throne and the living creatures

> *and the elders; and the number of them was*
> *myriads of myriads, and thousands of thousands,*
> *saying with a loud voice,*
> *"Worthy is the Lamb that was slaughtered to*
> *receive power, wealth, wisdom, might,*
> *honor, glory, and blessing."*
> *And I heard every created thing which is in*
> *heaven, or on the earth, or under the earth, or on*
> *the sea, and all the things in them, saying,*
> *"To Him who sits on the throne and to the Lamb*
> *be the blessing, the honor, the glory,*
> *and the dominion forever and ever."*
> *And the four living creatures were saying,*
> *"Amen." And the elders fell down and worshiped.*
>
> REVELATION 5:6-14 NASB

WITH TODAY BEING our last devotional, I thought we should look forward to our destiny. After all, if we don't have a clear idea of the direction we were meant to take, we'll wander aimlessly and might not reach the intended destination. But if we know who God planned for us to be, even if we are supremely under-qualified, we can take one step at a time toward that end goal. I think we can look at the rewards to the church's overcomers in Revelation 2-3 and get some good ideas of who we were created to be.

Recently I've been reading the beginning of Revelation over and over, and I came to realize a few things I didn't notice in previous readings. In all the ways Jesus told His churches to be a light on the earth as His golden lampstands, He had also accomplished ahead of us everything He asked that we do. He was able to encourage His churches and tell what blessings would come based on His own experience of what His Father had given Him.

For instance, here is one verse with two rewards mentioned:

*He who is able to hear, let him listen to and heed what the Spirit says to the assemblies (churches). To him who overcomes (conquers), I will give to eat of the manna that is hidden, and **I will give him a white stone with a new name engraved on the stone, which no one knows or understands except he who receives it**...*

REVELATION 2:17 AMPC
(EMPHASIS ADDED)

And seventeen chapters later, we see Jesus described as having received this same reward:

*Now I saw heaven opened, and behold, a white horse. And He who sat on him was called Faithful and True, and in righteousness He judges and makes war. His eyes were like a flame of fire, and on His head were many crowns. **He had a name written that no one knew except Himself.***

REVELATION 19:11-12 NKJV
(EMPHASIS ADDED)

Jesus had won the prizes declared for those who would hear, obey, and overcome by what the Spirit was saying. He was showing us the way. He doesn't direct as a king, who has never done the servant's work Himself.

Consider when He sent out His disciples, and gave them instructions in Matthew 10, He spoke prophetically what He would also do and endure ahead of them. He had already preached the kingdom of God and delivered those who were oppressed by the devil. And He knew He would be brought before judges, speak what the Spirit showed Him, and be scourged before taking up His literal cross (Matthew 10:16-39).

The Overcomer's Eternal Destiny

Let's highlight a few other awards Jesus spoke of:

> *"To all who are victorious, who obey me to the very end, to them **I will give authority over all the nations. They will rule** the nations with an iron rod and smash them like clay pots. **They will have the same authority I received from my Father**, and I will also give them the morning star! Anyone with ears to hear must listen to the Spirit and understand what He is saying to the churches...*
> *"Those who are victorious will **sit with Me on My throne, just as I was victorious and sat with My Father on His throne.**"*
> REVELATION 2:25-29
> AND 3:21 NLT
> (see also 1 Peter 2:9-10, Ephesians 2:1-10, and Colossians 3:1-4)

In previous devotionals, we recognized how we, as prodigals, returned to the Father and are seated in a special place of honor though we haven't deserved it. Remember, He doesn't intend for us to continue to act like we did when we were far from Him. He has seen past our weaknesses and planned for us to grow in maturity, character, and ability to handle this highest position. It's not just a "spiritual" honorary prize that only exists as we imagine scripture. Jesus is telling us how to actually be raised up and sit on His throne with Him.

We see in these verses again that Jesus has prepared the way for us to walk in His footsteps and receive invaluable rewards. Abba has destined us to be priests and kings and to rule with His Son throughout eternity (Revelation 5:10). Knowing this, we must change every mindset that hinders us from actually representing Him and manifesting His glory in the earth!

While we seek to expand the possibilities of what God could do through us, we must remain humble. This is not about gaining influence, acquiring a title, or building our own kingdoms. Even though Jesus is the King of kings and Lord of lords, He came as a servant. No matter how the Lord uses us, we must remember that we are just vessels, and the greatest way to lead is to serve.

And a dispute also developed among them as to which one of them was regarded as being the greatest. And He said to them, "The kings of the Gentiles domineer over them; and those who have authority over them are called 'Benefactors.' But it is not this way for you; rather, the one who is the greatest among you must become like the youngest, and the leader like the servant. For who is greater, the one who reclines at the table or the one who serves? Is it not the one who reclines at

> *the table? But I am among you as the one who serves.*
>
> *"You are the ones who have stood by Me in My trials; and just as My Father has granted Me a kingdom, I grant you that you may eat and drink at My table in My kingdom, and you will sit on thrones judging the twelve tribes of Israel.*
>
> LUKE 22:24-30 NASB
> (SEE ALSO LUKE 14:17-14)

Receiving a Heavenly Reward

Jesus was speaking specifically to His twelve disciples about the special positions they would have. Not because they were perfect; obviously, they had just been fighting over who was greatest among them! These were normal men—mainly fishermen and a tax collector. We read plenty about their doubts and mistakes throughout the New Testament, but their destinies were nearly immeasurable. They were rewarded because they did what Jesus taught them to do, and continued to obey His Spirit, no matter the cost.

> *Whether we live or die we make it our life's passion to live our lives pleasing to Him. For one day we will all be openly revealed before Christ on His throne so that each of us will be duly recompensed for our actions done in life, whether good or worthless.*
>
> 2 CORINTHIANS 5:6-10 TPT
> (see also Matthew 5:3-12, Matthew 6:19-34,
> Luke 12:13-48, Luke 16:8-13, Luke 19:11-27,

and 1 Timothy 6:17-19)

If the disciples could look back over their lives and give us a report, I'm sure they would say they tried to emulate Christ but made a lot of mistakes. Still, the Holy Spirit worked through them in amazing ways, bringing certain people across their paths and orchestrating their stories to accomplish His plans. And if we trace the faith lineage of what brought us to Christ, somewhere it touches these ordinary men's stories. They invested in eternity and received a priceless reward.

> *No one can lay any foundation other than the one we already have—Jesus Christ. Anyone who builds on that foundation may use a variety of materials—gold, silver, jewels, wood, hay, or straw. But on the judgment day, fire will reveal what kind of work each builder has done. The fire will show if a person's work has any value. If the work survives, that builder will receive a reward. But if the work is burned up, the builder will suffer great loss. The builder will be saved, but like someone barely escaping through a wall of flames.*
> 1 CORINTHIANS 3:11-15 NLT

Taking Steps Toward the Finish Line

It's better that His refining fire burns away the worthless parts of our lives now, than to get to the end of our stories and realize that we have no reward. We have this one opportunity. So we have to accurately judge where are now, and where we want to be. Let's do more than only think about if we will get to heaven, and consider the eternal value our lives are accruing.

When I read what Jesus told the churches in Revelation to do, I have to admit I'm not following perfectly. So I don't feel strong or that I have an identity as an overcomer. But I know that God would not ask me to do something that's impossible, and His Word is true even when I don't feel it. So by faith, I act as though I can do all things, I am more than a conqueror, and my faith is the victory that has overcome the world (Philippians 4:13, Romans 8:37, 1 John 5:4-5)!

We need to look forward and step into our destiny. We must live not only in the blessings of sonship, but also responsibility, as we steadily walk toward Jesus's throne. One day we will reach Him there, and our works will be judged. I pray after all is weighed in His perfect scales, that we are offered to sit with Him. Afterall, He is more than worthy of our lives. To Him who sits on the throne be the blessing, the honor, the glory, and the dominion forever and ever. He alone is worthy!

Pray today:

Abba, thank You for bringing me back to You and restoring me completely as Your child. I lay my life at Your feet again. Please help me to not think of it as my own. All the things I have pictured about what I would do, or even what following Jesus is about, I submit to You. I want to walk in the destiny of who You intended me to be. You thought of me and knew my days before one of them was written (Psalm 139:1-18). You have placed before me life and death and counseled me to choose life (Deuteronomy 30:19-20). You have planned to give me an incomprehensible future and hope (Jeremiah 29:11). Thank You!

Jesus, I want to follow in Your footsteps. Thank You for showing me the way. Thank You for going before me and leading me as a humble Master. You are gentle and meek, and You said Your burden is light (Matthew 11:28-30). Thank You for not only instructing me, but also that You understand my human frailty, because You humbled Yourself and came as a man (Hebrews 4:15). You lived in the power of the Holy Spirit and have given me the same Spirit and fire to also live as You did. You went ahead of me and are sharing the rewards that only You deserve. Thank You, thank You, thank You! Please help me to live a life worthy of the price You paid (1 Corinthians 6:19-20). I pray all of this in Your glorious name, Jesus! Amen!

Journaling prompt:

As you have been reading, did the Holy Spirit show you glimpses of what your future might hold? Dream with God, looking forward to your destiny in Christ, and write down what He shows you. You might also write down any other notes about what you received from these three weeks of devotionals.

_____
_____
_____
_____
_____

Rekindling the Fire

John W. Nichols

Additional Notes

I HOPE MY words have blessed you and encouraged you to return fully to the Father and who He created you to be. If they have, there are a few ways you can be even more blessed, forward the blessing to someone else, and help me at the same time. Check out all the free stuff I have for you below and find out how to partner with me and my family.

Who Needs to Hear this Message?

Take a moment and ask God to show you who else this book could help. He may bring someone to your mind who needs a fresh revelation of Abba's love. Or maybe someone who could take their faith in Christ deeper in order to change the world. This book would also be good for Bible study material.

If you or someone you know would like to go deeper in what it means to follow Christ and change the world, you should check out my series called Revival Fire-Starters. Find out more at:

GodAndYouAndMe.com/Fullness-of-Joy-Book

If you or someone you know is fighting for physical healing or would like to learn more about how to pray for healing, you should check out my book, Healing is Here. It is a 7-week devotional that shows God's will to heal and how to pray for it using Biblical examples. Find out more at:

GodAndYouAndMe.com/Healing-is-Here-Book

If you know someone who is going through a hard time, or struggling with questions about life and God, you can let them know they can get my ebook GOD is HERE, the accompanying workbook and journal, audiobook, and PDF on salvation and the gift of the Holy Spirit for free here:

GodAndYouAndMe.com/God-is-Here-Free-Stuff

Reviews are a Huge Help to Authors

Another way to help is with a few minutes of your time by leaving a quick review wherever you got this book. Reviews really help people to know if they should check out a book. You can review it on Amazon, Good Reads, Barnes & Noble, iBooks, Kobo, and/or Google Play Books. Please take a couple of minutes to review this book on one or more of these sites. I appreciate your feedback, so I can learn to communicate God's heart better, and hopefully reach more people. Thank you in advance!

More Free Books!

If you're interested in being an advance reader and have the opportunity to get future books for free, visit:

GodAndYouAndMe.com/Advance-Reader

Updates and Partnering with My Family

If you'd like an update on what God is doing with me and my family, and would like to support us in prayer or financially visit:

GodAndYouAndMe.com/Ministry-Partner

My Contact Information

Check out the About the Author section for a bit more info about me and my family, as well as how you can contact me, connect on social media, and receive encouraging blog posts on my website. I would love to hear any testimonies of the work that God has done in your life through this ministry. Please reach out!

FREE STUFF!

IF YOU HAVEN'T ALREADY be sure to download the free resources I've made available!

Free Stuff!

| Simple Steps to Hearing God | Walk with God, Change the World | Revolutionize Your Quiet Time |

Subscribe at: GodAndYouAndMe.com/rekindling-fire-free-stuff

Get These Free Resources

- *God is Trying to Tell You Something.* An audio teaching in MP3 format, focused on the key to hearing God, common ways God speaks, and practical steps to hear Him today.
- *7 Keys to a Successful Time of Devotion to God.* A PDF with steps to include in your quiet time.
- *Navigating the Maze of Life with God.* A 60 page

> PDF about giving your life to God, being filled with the Holy Spirit, and walking in the power of the Holy Spirit to live the life God intended you to live.

- Additional content only available to subscribers on GodAndYouAndMe.com. You can unsubscribe at any time and I promise not to spam you.

Get these free resources here. Most phones are capable of using the camera app to follow this link. Simply open the camera on your phone and point it at the page:

GodAndYouAndMe.com/Rekindling-Fire-Free-Stuff

ABOUT THE AUTHOR

JESUS RADICALLY SAVED John W. Nichols at the age of twenty. As a child he had loved to read and write, but drugs and alcohol had stolen his identity. Through the prayers and lives of a few people, he had a revelation of the love of God, and started reading His great love letter, the Holy Bible. As John laid everything down at Jesus's feet, his life was never the same.

He so wanted to serve the Lord, and give Him every talent. He thought one day (when he was old) he might write a book for God. But God thought he should write something sooner, and told John in a prayer session on January 1st, 2016, to write his book. Since then, John has written five books including the one you are reading.

In other prayer sessions, God called John to preach His Word, seek His face, and go into the land He would show Him. He and his wife, Trinna, and their three children, are following this call to show the love of Christ to the world. This was first exhibited teaching and leading worship in their local church, then by working with people with disabilities, then going to preach at the state prison, loving their neighborhood community, reaching out to women and children enslaved in human trafficking, making disciples of Jesus who will multiply, and now serving as missionaries in Rome, Italy.

When John caught a glimpse of how God saw him, everything changed, and he has since sought to show others this good news. He's recognized most people, Christian or not, feel unfulfilled and don't know their life's purpose. This has led John to help people find their calling and have a life of adventure with God. To be encouraged in the way God sees you, and to keep up with what God is doing with John and his family, go to:

You can also connect with John in the following ways.
Email:
John@GodAndYouAndMe.com
Short words of encouragement:
GodAndYouAndMe.com/Blog

Social Media:

Facebook.com/GodAndYouAndMeBlog

YouTube.com/channel/UCqG-TKZgn2PwwEQx9WlThoA

Istagram.com/Nichols_JohnW

Twitter.com/Nichols_JohnW

Linkedin.com/in/GodAndYouAndMe

GoodReads.com/author/show/18325435.John_W_Nichols

Amazon.com/author/Nichols_JohnW

www.ingramcontent.com/pod-product-compliance
Lightning Source LLC
Chambersburg PA
CBHW060559080526
44585CB00013B/622